THE
POLICE
SELECTION
PROCESS

THE
POLICE
SELECTION
PROCESS

3rd Edition

Ian Hutchison

ISP
CONSULTANCY

Publisher's Note

Every possible effort has been made to ensure that the information contained in this book is accurate at the time of going to press and the publishers and author cannot accept responsibility for any errors or omissions, however caused. No responsibility for loss or damage occasioned to any person acting, or refraining from action, as a result of the material in this publication can be accepted by the editor, the publisher or the author.

First published in Great Britain in 2007 entitled **The Police Selection Process**

First edition 2007 Second edition 2008 Third edition 2008

ISP Consultancy Ltd
1 Captains Gorse
Upper Basildon
Reading
RG8 8SZ
United Kingdom
www.ispconsultancy.com

British Library Cataloguing in Publication Data

A CIP record for this book is available from the British Library
ISBN 0-9554307-0-4

Printed and Bound in Great Britain by Lightning Source, Milton Keynes

Contents

ISP Consultancy Ltd.

ISP is a highly professional and experienced UK training organisation that offers comprehensive training for recruitment of Police Constables, Special Constables and Police Community Support Officers (PCSO).

We assist applicants who are considering a police career to develop skills that enables them to successfully complete the Application Form and the Assessment Centre stages of the selection process. After appointment as an officer we can assist you with your career and help you achieve progression to Specialist Departments and Promotion.

There is a support DVD for this book, which is available through the web site that demonstrates the Interactive Scenario and Competency Based Interview.

For further information about Courses, Seminars and One-to-One training see Appendix 7 and visit our web site:

www.ispconsultancy.com

Chapter 1

Introduction

Joining the police service today is nothing like it was when I joined in the mid 1970's. After a 'home visit' by a local sergeant in Cambridgeshire, where I was living at the time, I sat the Police Initial Recruitment Test that comprised Maths and English at Basingstoke Police Station.

Shortly after, I attended the Headquarters of Thames Valley Police for a day. The whole thing consisted of a group of budding recruits climbing aboard a Ford Transit van and travelling to a medical examination by the Police Surgeon in Beaumont Street, Oxford. We then returned for an interview with the Assistant Chief Constable.

I remember sitting in front of the desk and noticing that he seemed to do most of the talking, explaining what policing was about and how much he thought I would be suited. I cannot remember having to deal with any difficult questions. In fact, I recall he noted that I played the trumpet and should join the Force Band because they were short of players!

Even if you have only had a cursory look at what is now required you will know that things have changed a great deal for recruiting constables, police community support officers and special constables; but do not let that put you off!

Over 30 years ago the police service and society was different. The working conditions, the pay and the type of applicant were also different. With the passage of time the role of police officer in society has developed and become more complex. In consequence, the job has attracted a wider range of applicants and individual police forces have responded by developing bespoke selection processes to identify the right people. Only a few years ago you would have discovered a different approach to selection across the 55 forces in the British Isles.

Today, nationally, there are in excess of 30,000 applicants to the police service each year. Clearly, the police have the opportunity to select the best of the bunch and consequently only around 6% get selected (about 5,000) for a police career.

The Home Office recently introduced a National Recruitment Model (NRM) to standardise the approach to recruiting.

Stage 1, the Application Form, requires you to submit personal details to enable the police to judge whether you meet the basic entry requirements. It also has competency based questions which are assessed to determine whether you have sufficient life experience to progress to the next stage. If you fail here you will have to wait six months before you can reapply.

Stage 2, the Assessment Centre, requires you to undergo a series of tests comprising numerical and verbal reasoning, written exercises, interactive scenarios and an interview.

Stage 3, the Physical Fitness and Medical, is designed to test whether you are fit enough to undertake the rigours of police work. If you pass this stage you will receive an offer of appointment as a police constable in your chosen force.

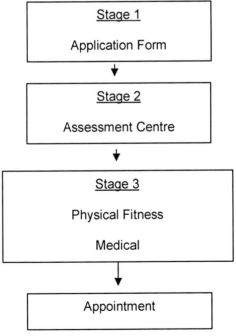

This book has two objectives. Firstly, to give you a clear picture of what is required as you progress through the selection process and, secondly, to show you how to prepare yourself properly. There is a plethora of information about 'what' the police do and the criteria required to join but there is very little good advice about 'how' to prepare for the challenge.

As you flick through the chapters in this book you will realise that it has a 'no nonsense' approach. Each exercise you will have to undertake during the selection process is fully explained and you are provided with a methodology for dealing with each one.

This is not based on some 'insider' information about the process; it is a direct result of personal experience of undertaking similar assessment exercises. It is also based on recognised development techniques and experience of coaching people into different professions, including many successful police recruits.

There is also a DVD accompanying this book that demonstrates the methodology for dealing with the interactive scenarios and the competency based interview. You may find this useful in understanding what is required.

There is no magic to personal success contained in these pages. You will make your own luck. As Confucius profoundly articulated:

"Tell me and I will forget;
Show me and I may remember;
Involve me and I'll understand."

If you want to make your own luck and be successful in getting through the police selection process you must understand what is required and then follow a practical development programme that will enhance your skills and prepare you for the role of police constable.

Take for example a customer services job in a large department store. If someone told you what the job is about, would you be able to do it? If they demonstrated the job with a real life customer, would the job be clearer? If you had a go at dealing with an angry customer yourself, would you have a better understanding of the job and would you be any good at it? If you actually have a go at the job you would certainly understand it better and, if you do it time after time, you will become really good at it. There is no substitute for real life experience.

So, the philosophy of this development programme is simple. Once you know what is required you do it and then practice, practice, practice. Your personal skills will rapidly improve as a result.

With this in mind you should be prepared to work hard to achieve your ambition. The information contained in this book will help you to understand what is required and give you the tools to do the job, but you will need to translate that into real skills development. Through this process you will be prepared for the challenge of the selection process and the old adage of the six 'P's' will ring true:

'Prior Preparation and Planning Prevents Poor Performance'

The chapters in this book are designed to give you everything you will need to get you through each stage of the process and ensure your learning is progressive. You are given information when you need it without overload or confusion. That way you will not be intimidated by the process or question your ability to get through. Each chapter is also a stand-alone information source that you can dip into to deal with specific issues.

Beginning with the Application Form, you will be introduced to the complexity of the information required and the importance of the competency based questions in Section 4. After that there is an overview of the National Policing Improvement Agency (NPIA) selection process and the information you will be supplied with before attending the Assessment Centre.

After that, you will be introduced to the seven core competencies required for the role of constable and, importantly, how you can match yourself against them.

This is very important as you are aspiring to become a police officer and the skills that you have must match what is required of the job.

Once you have learned how to match your skills to the role you will be introduced to the Competency Based Interview. You will be demonstrating your understanding of four core competencies through answering questions that require you to give real life examples of occasions where you have demonstrated the competencies. The remaining exercises in the Assessment Centre will then be addressed. You will learn how to deal with the Written Exercises and the Interactive Scenarios using a tried and tested structured approach. There is a chapter on Interview Technique for those candidates who may have to attend a force filter interview in addition to the NRM. Finally, there is general advice and guidance about the preparation process.

By the time you have been through each of the chapters you will have a good idea of what is required and how you will need to develop yourself to achieve the standard required. Most applicants will use this book to confirm that they have many of the skills required and be able to demonstrate them at the Assessment Centre. That is a positive outcome and a solid basis on which to take your ambition forward.

If you have real doubts about whether you can achieve the standard required or not, that is also a solid basis on which to proceed. Seek advice and it may be that a short period of focused development will deal with issues that will then make you more confident in taking your application forward.

Whether you are reading this book as part of your general information gathering process because you are interested in a police career or you are a seriously committed applicant you will find that it provides everything you need to prepare for success.

Good luck with your police career.

Ian Hutchison
January 2007

Note to 3rd Edition:
In response to the growing use of 'filter interviews' by police forces as an additional component to the NRM I have included a section on *Interview Technique* at chapter 10 to help candidates prepare.

Ian Hutchison
June 2008

Chapter 2

Completing the Application Form

The Application Form is Stage 1 of the selection process. It requires you to provide a considerable amount of personal information to enable the police to determine whether you fit the recruitment criteria and if you have the life experience to progress to Stage 2, the Assessment Centre. You should be clear that the application is an integral part of the assessment process and if you fail to pass this stage you will have to wait six months before you can reapply.

After you have submitted the completed Application Form to your chosen force it is likely you will be sent a formal acknowledgement that it has been received by the recruiting department. It will then be checked to make sure it has been completed properly and that you fit the minimum criteria to become a police officer. For example, it will be necessary to check that you fit the residency rule. They will then mark your competency based questions and carry out vetting and reference checks.

The procedure differs from one police force to another so it is important that you check with your chosen force what the procedure is to prevent personal anxiety and unnecessary telephone calls to the recruiting department about the progress of your application. Some forces carry out the marking, vetting and reference checks before they notify you that you have been successful at Stage 1. This can take some time, occasionally up to three months. If you are aware of this you will be able to rest easy knowing that no news is good news!

The Application Form

It goes without saying that you must take the greatest care in completing the Application Form and, in particular, formulating your answers to the four competency based questions in Section 4. If you do not take time to produce a good application you will not get through Stage 1 first time.

At the back of the application form there are 'Guidance notes for the completion of this Application Form' that should be read carefully. It is also a good idea to rehearse your responses to the various sections on rough paper in draft format to make sure you have composed them correctly, rather than insert them immediately and spoil the application. This is not a document that should be completed in one evening at first attempt. Draft up your responses and then return to them over a period of days to see how you can improve on the content, spelling, punctuation and grammar.

Your application can be made in traditional hard copy format or electronically through the Police Could You? Web site(www.policecouldyou.co.uk).

If you decide to use the web site you must check whether your chosen force will permit an application in this format. Some forces insist on a handwritten hard copy. Either way, the principles for completion remain the same.

Section 1 - About You

This is an important section that asks you to provide a broad range of information about yourself that includes personal details, the force you are applying to, disabilities, nationality, convictions and cautions, tattoos, membership of the British National Party (BNP) or similar, health, eyesight and disability, business interests, financial position, previous addresses and about your family.

All of this information will be used to determine whether you fit the basic conditions for entry to the police service. If you fail to meet the criteria, for example, residency, previous convictions or basic health requirements then the force reserves the right to not progress your application. To avoid disappointment it is recommended that you read the Entry Criteria (Appendix 4) before you submit an application and if there is any doubt in your mind check with your chosen force whether they are prepared to accept an application from you in the particular circumstances.

Section 2 - About Your Employment

This section is seeking information about your work record and asks questions about your present or most recent employment, previous employment, referees, service in Her Majesty's (HM) Forces and previous applications to or service with a police force.

The information you provide in this section will be used to determine your level of motivation in the work place. Your work record will demonstrate how long you have been in employment, why you decided to move from one job to another and the positions that you held. References will be checked and therefore it is a good idea to approach prospective referees and ask for consent to put their names forward. It is also a good idea to know how they see you and what they might say in response to a request for a reference.

If you have served with HM Forces you should provide information about your service number, your commanding officer and unit details. The police will use this information to verify your service record, your discharge date and reserve liabilities. If you have previously served as a police officer, special constable, support staff or cadet the police will be interested to know about your time working for the police force.

It is important that you present a good work record. Long periods of unemployment or a high level of accumulated frequent sickness, that cannot be justified, are likely to raise questions in the mind of any employer, let alone the police who require a high level of motivation and commitment. If you fall into that category make sure you can justify your position or do something to put it right before you apply.

Section 3 - About Your Education and Skills

This section is intended to give the police a view of your education record, academic achievements and other skills you possess. There are no formal academic requirements for entry to the police service but the skills required, including numerical and verbal reasoning, are tested at Stage 2, the Assessment Centre. However, the police want to know where you were educated and what qualifications you have attained in recognised academic subjects as well as vocational and professional subjects. Make sure that you tell the police about voluntary work and charitable initiatives that you have been involved with. These demonstrate you have a broader perspective on life and enable you to make a valuable contribution as a police officer. Your ability to speak languages is also important as these skills may be utilised by the force during your service. You could find yourself involved on a special investigation if you can speak another language. Make sure that you use this opportunity to demonstrate your achievements and present a full picture of what you have to offer.

Section 4 - Competency Assessment

This is a very important section of the application form and a great deal of thought and care should be taken during the preparation of your answers. The first four questions are 'competency based questions' (CBQ) requiring you to provide answers that demonstrate you have the basic life experiences and skills to enable your progression to the Assessment Centre stage. After submitting your application the answers are 'marked' and graded 'A', 'B', 'C' or 'D'. To pass the application stage you will have to attain a grade 'B', or higher, overall. As indicated above if you fail at this stage of the process you will have to wait six months before you can reapply.

How to Answer the Questions

The questions require you to provide examples of **'what'** and **'how'** you did certain things in different situations. Your answers to the questions must be examples from your personal life experience. There must be a focus on what **you did** in a particular situation. It is no good saying what you **knew** or **thought** about things. They are looking for **your** actions.

You will not score well if there is any confusion over what you did as opposed to what others **did** and **said**. Generalisations, like **'we'**, rather than **'I'**, are not clear in demonstrating what you did and will not score well.

You must provide the detail about a particular initiative and be clear which things you were personally responsible for doing.

The competency based questions that are asked will vary from time to time as do the interactive scenarios, application form and other aspects of the process. However, the principles outlined above are good for any question asked.

The examples that follow demonstrate typical answers to questions for Respect for Race and Diversity and Personal Responsibility.

Example 1 - Respect for Race and Diversity

Demonstrating that you can respect the lifestyle, culture or beliefs of others even if these differed significantly from your own views.

'When I met my wife I discovered she was a devout Roman Catholic. I was Church of England, not very religious and I could not understand why she was so devoted because I had not been brought up that way. The whole thing became an issue when we decided to get married. She wanted to marry in the Catholic Faith in the local Catholic Church. I disagreed with the strength of her belief and I was happy to marry in a Register Office.

I found the strength of her belief, and that of her family, to be excessive because my faith was not as strong and I could not see why it should be such a big issue. I also felt that the issue of religion was going to cause difficulties between us and ruin a good relationship and a happy future.

I decided to deal with the issues and attended a series of ten lessons with the local Catholic Priest to learn about the Catholic Faith. This enabled me to understand the commitment of my wife and her family to the marriage taking place in the Catholic Church. Also, this enabled me to understand the strength of her belief. As a result I was happy to get married in the Catholic Church and effectively be inducted into the faith. Since getting married both our children have been baptised in the Catholic Faith and I support their beliefs.

It is important that beliefs do not get in the way of living harmoniously. I adapted to her beliefs by learning about and becoming inducted into the faith.

Example 2 - Personal Responsibility

Demonstrating that you can take personal responsibility for getting things done without having to be told.

'My neighbours were due to move house one Friday morning.

They were both in their 70's. The new residents arrived at 12 noon to take over the house with their removal van to find that my neighbours had not moved out as they should by that time. The new residents were being very aggressive to the elderly couple who were becoming increasingly upset and distressed. I decided to see what the problem was.

It appeared that the removal firm had failed to confirm the booking. They had, therefore, not turned up to move the elderly couple. I decided to intervene and sort out the problem.

I calmed the new residents and said I would take responsibility for sorting things out. I then obtained the assistance of a friend and obtained two vans. We them moved all of the couple's property out of the house and transferred it to their new house. It was late at night when it was completed but we made the couple comfortable ensuring they had a bed to sleep in and the other necessary comforts were available to them. They were very pleased as were the new residents who were able to move into their new home.'

There are a number of other questions that follow the CBQ and ask why you want to become a police officer, why you want to join the force to which you are applying, what tasks you expect to be undertaking as a police officer, what impact police work will have on your social and domestic life, and what you have done to prepare yourself to become a police officer.

It is important that you are clear what these questions are asking and you provide full answers that demonstrate you have researched the role of police constable and you understand the unique nature of the work. In answer to the question,

'What is the job of a police officer?'

It is no good answering this question by saying that,

> *'I will be working in the community'*

> *'I will be helping people'*

These answers are not specific enough and do not demonstrate you know what the job is about and you have clear expectations of what you will be dealing with. A better response to this question would include the following:

'I will be working shifts and be deployed on foot and mobile patrols to prevent and detect crimes. I will be dealing with theft, assault, burglary, sexual offences, cases of sudden death, road collisions, giving evidence in court, dealing with paperwork, drunkenness, public disorder and anything else that I am required to deal with'.

This answer is much more specific and demonstrates your understanding of the role of constable. All of your answers to these questions should be prepared to the same standard. The fact that these questions are not marked like the CBQ does not mean that they should be treated as if they are of less importance.

Summary

It is extremely important to spend as much time as possible thinking about what you are going to write on the Application Form. Use photocopies of the form to draft up your responses and only when you are completely satisfied with the product should you fill in the form.

This is especially important where the competency based questions are concerned. You must make sure your answers are in line with the questions asked and demonstrate the competency required. You may have to draft and re-draft several times to get them right. Between reviews of your answers get someone to read them through for you and provide you with constructive feedback that will help you improve them. Only when you are totally confident they are up to the required standard should you submit the form. Remember a little time spent now may prevent a six month wait before you can reapply.

Chapter 3

Briefing Information for Candidates

After passing Stage 1 of the process, you will be notified of the intended date for your appearance before the Assessment Centre. About two or three weeks before the date you will receive two NPIA documents that provide you with essential briefing information. These documents are:

1. Structured Entrance Assessment for Recruiting Constables Holistically - Information for Candidates

2. The Westshire Centre - Welcome Pack

These documents are very important and essential reading for anyone who is going forward to the assessment stage. The documents are very open and intended to provide the information you will need to prepare for the day. The documents honestly state what you will have to deal with and there is no hidden agenda. If you understand the information you will have no surprises on the day. In fact, it is important to recognise that the assessment centre process is intended to be transparent and to treat everyone equally and fairly.

Overview of the Documents

1. Structured Entrance Assessment for Recruiting Constables Holistically - Information for Candidates

This is a comprehensive document that is intended to provide you with information about the selection process and what can be expected on the day. What follows is an overview of some of the key information provided.

(a) Introduction

At the outset the information makes clear that when you attend the Assessment Centre you will be there for about five hours. You should consider bringing a snack with you that can be taken during the breaks between exercises. It also states that you will need to bring a passport or two other documents specified in a list, to prove your identity.

(b) What is an Assessment Centre?

In line with the 'openness' mentioned above the document describes what an Assessment Centre is, the historical context to its use and the competencies that will be used to test people attending the centre.

(c) What exercises will you have to undertake?

You will be required to undertake a competency based structured interview that will last 20 minutes during which you will have to answer four questions, a numerical reasoning test lasting 12 minutes, a verbal logical reasoning test lasting 25 minutes, two written exercises lasting 20 minutes each and four interactive scenarios lasting 5 minutes each. These exercises are explained in some detail to give you a clear picture of what you can expect.

It is also explained that for the written exercises and four interactive scenarios you will be in role as a Customer Services Officer at a shopping centre called 'The Westshire Centre'. This is a fictitious shopping centre created for the purposes of the Assessment Centre and all the information you will need to know about it is contained in the 'Westshire Centre Welcome Pack'.

Following this, there is comprehensive information about what can be expected during the various tests, who are the assessors and what information they have about you before the day.

It is important to recognise that the assessors, who run the centre to a set of pre-determined guide lines, will only know your candidate number and will not have any other information about you. You should be reassured by this that the process is objective and fair.

(d) How am I assessed?

You will be assessed against the seven core competencies and the exercises you will have to undertake are designed to test your skills. You will be tested at least three times in each competency except for Respect for Race and Diversity that is tested seven times. A grading will be awarded on a scale from A to D. Grade A is awarded to the best performing candidates and D to the least strong performing candidates.

(e) The timetable

It is important that you arrive promptly at the time allocated for your assessment. If you are late you may be unable to undertake the assessment and, depending on what your chosen force decides, you may have to reapply. So, do not be late. Whether you are scheduled for a morning or afternoon assessment you will be there for about 5 hours. You will join a small group of other candidates and move around the exercises together. Other groups of candidates will be undertaking exercises at the same time.

(f) How to prepare for the exercises

This is a very useful section on how you can prepare for the exercises. In the Competency Based Interview, Interactive Scenarios and

Written Exercises it advocates matching your skills against the seven core competencies and enlist the help of colleagues, friends or family to help you. This is covered fully in chapter 5.

There is also good advice on how you should prepare for the Numerical Reasoning and Verbal Logical Reasoning tests. There are some practice tests in the document to give you an idea of what to expect. It even tells you not to worry if you do not finish the tests as many candidates are unable to complete all the questions. This is dealt with in chapter 9.

(g) Advance information on the exercises

This extremely useful section outlines the information you have in advance about each exercise. This is very helpful as it is quite detailed and gives you a good idea of what you will have to do. For example, in one of the written exercises, "...you will be required to write a Proposal Document regarding an issue between two stores at the Westshire Centre." The detail in this statement, combined with the fact that the Welcome Pack contains a Proposal Document Template and a job description for the Customer Services Officer that refers to preparing reports, is giving you a very strong message about what will be required of you. I think from this you can assume you will be writing a report for someone. This is dealt with in chapter 8.

(h) Core competencies

Finally, this document provides a full breakdown of the seven core competencies. Overall, there is a considerable amount of information contained in this briefing document.

It should all be considered in great detail. If, at first, it seems very complicated, try to absorb the process of the Assessment Centre and then focus on the exercises you will have to deal with. In this way you will be able to concentrate your thoughts on exactly what you will have to deal with. Look closely for clues as to what you are likely to have to do, as discussed at (g) above.

2. The Westshire Centre - Welcome Pack

The Welcome Pack is essential reading and should form a key part of your preparation for the Assessment Centre. It is directly linked to the problems you will have to deal with in the Interactive Scenarios and Written Exercises. Think of the document as a jigsaw puzzle. It contains all of the 'pieces' of information that you will need to assist you in the exercises. The only 'piece' you will not have is the problem presented by the briefing information and role actors in the exercises. However, if you are familiar with the information in the Welcome Pack you will soon be able to complete the picture.

For the purpose of the Interactive Scenarios and

Written Exercises you will be in role as a newly appointed Customer Services Officer at the Westshire Centre. This is a fictitious shopping centre which has 156 retail units, many of which are high street chain stores. The Welcome Pack contains briefing information that new employees are given, prior to commencing employment, to provide them some idea of their job and the organisation in which they will be working.

This is explained in the introduction to the pack and lists the documents that are included. For example, there may be documents on Centre Information, Operations Department, Customer Services – Main Duties and Responsibilities, Proposal Document, Equality Policy Statement, Lost Person Policy and Parking Policy for Parent and Child Parking.

Study the pack and assume that all the information provided is relevant. Look for links between pieces of information. For example, in the list of Main Duties and Responsibilities for Customer Services Officer there is a reference to completing "...accurate written reports of incidents, events and suggested resolutions to problems as and when required (please see the Proposal Document Template overleaf)". Clearly, as you know, you must write two proposal documents. This is a good clue as to what you will have to deal with and the format that you will use. Also, there is a mention of "safeguarding lost children". This is a trigger to look very carefully at the Lost Person Policy, if there is one. You should know what it says and what the procedure is for dealing with lost people, particularly children. In fact, you should examine all the policies in detail. The parking policy for parent and child states it is, "In line with The Westshire Centre's Equality Policy Statement..." Ask yourself what that means; perhaps you should be familiar with that policy as well.

As you prepare yourself for the Interactive Scenarios and Written Exercises use the Welcome Pack to inform your thinking. Think of problems and issues that you might have to deal with in the context of the Westshire Centre then apply the information and policies to them.

To illustrate the point, here are some typical scenarios you might have to deal with in the exercises:

1. Mrs. Lamb, a lady in her 80's became separated from her daughter during a shopping trip to the Westshire Centre. When she approached a security officer for assistance he was dismissive and rude to her. She wishes to complain about the behaviour of the security officer.

2. Mrs. Wong was walking past two men working on the escalator. One of them made comments to Mrs. Wong about her oriental features. She is most upset by the comments and requires some action against the man.

Summary

Success at the Assessment Centre depends on the quality of your preparation. Make sure that the information provided by NPIA, particularly the 'Westshire Centre Welcome Pack', forms a key part of a structured approach to your development programme. You should begin to think like a Customer Services Officer and work out how you will deal with problems that might arise. You will certainly have a different view of your local shopping centre the next time you visit.

Chapter 4

Core Competencies

During your research into the role of a police officer you will have already discovered the demanding and varied nature of the work. The day-to-day demands of policing will call on all the skills you possess and stretch you beyond the limits of what is normally expected of citizens in society. Still, you wanted a challenge and that is what you will get!

Such is the demanding nature of policing it is extremely important that the police service recruits people who possess the skills to deal with the vast array of 'routine' matters that most members of the public would not even dream of dealing with.

Consequently, the police service is looking for an eclectic group of people who come from all walks of life and have different experiences to bring to policing. You will not lose your personality when you join the service, you will be trained to be a police officer and all of your other life experiences will enrich the person you become.

However, you must possess the basic skills that include physical and morale courage, integrity, leadership, team working, communication, resilience, flexibility, sensitivity to individual needs and many more. Following extensive research into the role of police officer the required vocational skills have been defined as the seven 'Core Competencies Relevant to the Role of Police Constable'.

As indicated in chapter 3, you will receive a list of the core competencies as an appendix to the NPIA document, 'Structured Entrance Assessment for Recruiting Constables Holistically – Information to Candidates'. These seven competencies are used in the Assessment Centre to test whether candidates reach the required standard for entry to the police service and whether you possess the necessary potential to develop into an efficient and effective constable through the probationary training period.

As you undertake the various exercises on the assessment day you will be marked against a matrix of core competencies on which you will have to score the prescribed overall mark to pass the selection process. The pass mark varies across police forces. Generally it is 60% but some have lowered it to 55% and 50%. The competencies are applied to the exercises to test the range of skills required and are graded A (3), B (2), C (1) and D (0). The numbers in the brackets are the scores awarded to each of the grades and your overall mark is based on the total scores accumulated during the process.

There is no need to worry unduly about which competencies you will be tested against in specific exercises.

You should concentrate on being yourself and producing a consistent tailored performance across all of them to ensure you score good marks. If you prepare properly you will be ready for the challenge.

You do, however, need to be aware that there are three competencies where you must score a minimum mark. If you do not achieve the minimum score in any one of them you will fail the assessment, even if you have achieved an overall mark above the prescribed pass mark. The competencies are:

- Respect for Race and Diversity (60%)
- Oral Communication (60%)
- Written Communication (44%)

These competencies are considered fundamental to the role of police officer. For example, Respect for Race and Diversity is considered so important that it is tested in all of the exercises except numerical and verbal logical reasoning tests. Clearly, this is an area that you will need to understand and be aware of the breadth of the subject. You should also make sure you understand how to apply diversity to all the exercises.

The Competencies

It is clear from what has been said above that your knowledge and understanding of the core competencies is paramount. They are pivotal to the process and the exercises you will be undertaking.

It cannot be emphasised too much just how important it is to understand each of the competencies and your feelings, views and behaviours in each one. The following chapter will deal in more detail with a process for matching yourself to the competencies and help you understand your position in relation to each one.

To assist your understanding of the competencies here is an overview.

1. Community and Customer Focus

'Focuses on the customer and provides a high quality service that is tailored to meet their individual needs. Understands the communities that are served and shows an active commitment to policing that reflects their needs and concerns'

As a police officer you will be dealing with people from different backgrounds, cultures, religious beliefs and intellectual ability. It is important that an officer understands the principles of diversity as outlined in the competency Respect for Race and Diversity and the requirement to provide everyone with a tailored service which meets their needs.

The focus on the customer is fundamental to the work of a police officer. This competency is looking for an understanding that the role requires a real commitment to providing a high quality tailored service for individuals and an understanding of the need to pursue principles of policing that reflect their needs and is responsive to them. In addition, it is also about how you support the aims and strategies of an organisation to promote a credible image that demonstrates commitment to customers and communities.

A quick look at the positive and negative indicators provides a clear picture of the behaviours that are required. You will need to think of an occasion where you provided a high level of customer service that required on-going contact and resolution of problems which resulted in a satisfactory outcome for the customer. You will also need to think of an occasion or a series of events where you did things that showed your commitment to the aims and objectives of the organisation and its positive impact on society. A good tip in demonstrating this competency is to make sure you focus on the customer and always try to learn from the problem the person has experienced and use the learning to improve how things are dealt with in future for the common good.

2. Effective Communication

'Communicates ideas and information effectively, both verbally and in writing. Uses language and a style of communication that is appropriate to the situation and people being addressed. Makes sure that others understand what is going on'

You will have noted above that Oral Communication and Written Communication are two competency areas that you will have to pass with 60% and 44%, respectively, to ensure a pass at the Assessment Centre. They are both skill areas that are contained within this competency and are very important to the role of police officer.

The ability to recognise that there are different people in society is important. But the ability to communicate effectively across the range of abilities, for example, with people of high intellect and those who have learning difficulties, is essential. It goes further and includes sensitivities to people who have disabilities or do not speak English. Being able to communicate verbally and using the written word appropriate to individual need is important.

When speaking to people it is important to use words and phrases that they will understand. Try to speak clearly using simple uncomplicated statements. Obviously, the ability to tailor your oral communication will be driven by who you are speaking to. Talking to an academic will be different to speaking to a vagrant, or will it?

You should be able to recognise quickly the level at which you will have to communicate to get the message across. When you have done so you should be able to handle individual and group encounters with confidence. You should also have the ability to summarise information to check that people understand the position.

Police officers are well known for having to produce a considerable amount of paper work in the course of their duties.

This is largely connected with the investigation of offences and the production of case papers for court proceedings. It is essential that you have the ability to take statements from witnesses, using language and words they will understand, and, when it comes to seeking advice and summarising facts for lawyers, you have the ability to summarise information, arguments and recommendations effectively. There also has to be a simple and well structured approach to your written work.

Effective communication is all of the above, but it should be recognised that the art of communication consists of other factors. Firstly, listening carefully to what people say is very important. Secondly, checking the facts by asking questions is fundamental to understanding the problem. By doing these two things you will complement the other skills required to ensure that quality interactive communication takes place.

3. Personal Responsibility

'Takes personal responsibility for making things happen and achieving results. Displays motivation, commitment, perseverance and conscientiousness. Acts with a high degree of integrity'

This competency is fairly self explanatory and is easily understood by taking a look at the positive indicators. In simple terms, the police service is looking for well motivated people who are prepared to go out of their way to get things done, without having to be asked. A police officer is expected to recognise what is required and to get on and deal with it. You will not wait for your sergeant to invite or tell you to deal with something. It will be expected. A police officer is not the kind of person that looks the other way when something occurs, they should take the initiative and deal with the situation.

Your example for this competency will show that you saw that something needed to be done. It might be a problem at work, a road accident or a person who was taken ill in the street. Having recognised action was required, you responded by taking the initiative and dealt with the situation. The most important behavioural trait is that you took responsibility for your actions and you did everything to a very high standard. Enthusiasm, positive attitudes and a desire to learn new skills and gain experience are also key to the competency.

Of course, there is also a requirement that you are open, honest and show integrity through your initiative. Finally, you should show that you are highly motivated in dealing with other people's problems and it is not just for your own self-interest.

4. Problem Solving

'Gathers information from a range of sources. Analyses information to identify problems and issues, and makes effective decisions'

A considerable amount of a police officer's time is spent solving a whole range of different problems for members of the public. Sometimes this involves neighbour disputes, youths causing nuisance on street corners or matters connected with crime. Police forces across the country frequently engage with the community to assist them with problem solving which often features 'hot spot' problem locations.

A simple real life example of a police 'problem' was a car park at a motorway service station that had been plagued with thefts from motorist's parked cars who are visiting the services. An inspection of the location revealed that a six feet hedge lying between the car park and the front of the service station obscured the view of the car park from the restaurant. Officers considered the hedge was the problem by providing cover for criminals whilst they broke into cars.

The hedge was cut down to three feet and the view of the car park was reinstated. Immediately the thefts from cars ceased. This case illustrates a problem solving approach. There are many more complex problems than this and some are major crime prevention initiatives to reduce crime and the fear of crime on large housing estates.

Whatever the problem, the solution must address the root causes. In the example given it was the hedge. Now consider the case of a dripping tap. There are two ways of dealing with it. Firstly, deal with the symptoms by turning the tap off tighter to stop the dripping or, secondly, strip the tap down to find out whether the washer and seating are in good order. If they are not, treat the problem by re-cutting the seat and replacing the washer to stop the dripping.

So, by understanding these principles you can begin to see what the competency is looking for. By employing a simple problem solving model like SARA – Searching, Analysing, Responding and Assessing, we can begin to build a structured approach and see how the positive indicators become relevant to the competency.

> **S**earching - When you perceive you have a problem it is important that you look at it carefully, from all angles, to confirm this is an issue that needs resolving.

> **A**nalysing – when you have confirmed there is a problem it is important to carry

out an analysis to establish the root causes. You must dig deep into the problem by examining information, documents, speaking to people and looking at the knock-on effects and how it impacts on other systems and processes.

Responding – this is about making an informed decision about what is to be done to resolve the problem and putting in place measures and changes to deal with the issues. The actions you take should deal with the causes of the problem rather than just treating the symptoms.

Assessing – after the measures have been put in place it is important to check that the decisions that have been made deal with the issues effectively. Follow up checks must be made to ensure the causes of the problem have been eliminated.

You should note that problem solving and team working are not mutually exclusive and work well together.

5. Resilience

'Shows resilience, even in difficult circumstances. Prepared to make difficult decisions and has the confidence to see them through'

Police officers routinely have to deal with trauma. Confronting armed and dangerous criminals, attending serious road collisions, dealing with domestic disputes, arresting violent drunken youths and dealing with incidents of sudden death are just some examples of where resilience is important. It is a very challenging experience to deal with a sudden death at a person's home and being surrounded by highly emotional relatives. You will have a very important investigation to carry out and it is essential that you remain calm, think clearly and put to one side your own emotions.

It is often times like this when you have to show morale and physical courage to overcome the pressure that will be put upon you to change your mind or deviate from the course of action you have to follow. You must be strong enough to fend off the pressure and make the right decisions.

Whatever the situation, as a police officer, you must remain calm, never get flustered, stay in control and resist the temptation to rush to a decision just because it will be more comfortable to do so. Sometimes your decisions will be unpopular or controversial but you must stand by your decision providing you feel it is right to do so.

As you consider the behaviours required by this competency you should think of a time when you had to deal with something that was difficult for you. You may have had to deal with a situation that was highly emotional or particularly difficult to resolve. Perhaps you had to deal with a frightening situation with a drunken customer, you were involved in a road collision, you had to deal with a serious illness in the family, or you had to deal with an aggressive customer who was complaining about a defective product. Whatever the experience is, examine the positive indicators carefully and identify the behaviours that you demonstrated during the course of the events.

6. Respect for Race and Diversity

'Considers and shows respect for the opinions, circumstances and feelings of colleagues and members of the public, no matter what their race, religion, position, background, circumstances, status or appearance'

Police officers set standards in the community, largely because they are dealing with people and because they are the instruments of strong political will to move towards an integrated and tolerant society. Recent years have seen much greater acceptance of issues that, in the past, were unacceptable to many people. So, issues of sexuality, race, religion, age and disability have been dealt with head-on.

The report by Sir William McPherson QC (1997) into the death of Stephen Lawrence dealt with many of these issues. The most interesting outcome of the report was 'Institutional Racism'. There was a recognition that society had to change from the established rigid approaches of the past where wittingly or unwittingly we excluded minority groups. We must move to a more flexible and inclusive acceptance of all diverse groups in society.

The position before McPherson was one of treating people 'equally'. By applying the same standards to all people we will exclude certain groups. For example, working practices that do not allow a Muslim to pray at different times of the day or a company that refuses to employ disabled people in wheelchairs. The position now is that we must have a flexible and fair approach. We must do positive things to include everyone and provide opportunities for all.

The competency requires you to understand this and to be sensitised to people's needs and beliefs. Diversity is now a broad subject and includes race, religion, cultural beliefs, sexuality, age, disability, size, personal beliefs on abortion, fox hunting, and almost any subject where tolerance and understanding are required. The only caveat on tolerance is criminality. Clearly, criminality cannot be tolerated and it is important to recognise where the boundaries lie.

Police officers need to demonstrate their tolerance and understanding by treating people with respect, showing concern for their problems, making them feel valued, understanding social customs and challenging attitudes and behaviours that are abusive, aggressive and discriminatory. The positive indicators clearly lay out what kind of behaviour you should be demonstrating and if you look at the negative indicators you will see the contrast. For example, 'Using behaviour inappropriately', 'Shows little understanding of the cultural and religious beliefs of different cultures' and 'Does not consider other people's feelings'. It becomes clear what is required for this competency.

7. Team Working

'Develops strong working relationships inside and outside the team to achieve common goals. Breaks down barriers between groups and involves others in discussions and decisions.'

This competency is looking for an understanding of team working principles and how well you work in the team environment. You should understand the basic principles of team working like recognising that a team is greater, or better, at solving problems and dealing with issues than any one individual and that an effective team is made up of different people with complementary skills.

It is also looking to see if you understand that you can be a member of different teams that are mutually supportive.

Apart from the basic principles, they are looking to see how you work in a team. Police officers frequently work in teams, sometimes at short notice, with people that you may not have worked with before. It is an essential skill area for potential police officers to be able to demonstrate. Being focused on achieving team objectives, even if there is no personal gain, is an important aspect of team working, as is the ability to strike up relationships with other people, contribute ideas, help others solve problems and always be approachable. You should also know your preferred role in a team. Are you an ideas person, do you like to be the leader, are you happy to do any task or are you the kind of person who seeks out and obtains resources for the benefit of the team?

To help you discover these team working traits you need to think of an occasion when you worked in a team and then use the example to describe the process that the team adopted to show you understand the team working principles. Then you will need to say how you and the other members interacted and worked together to get the task completed. Team working, like problem solving, requires a process model that enables you to demonstrate the skills required. We shall use the model ASSAD.

Analysing - When the team comes together to deal with the task the members must establish the position they are in. It is important to recognise what information, resources, support mechanisms and specialist skills you have amongst the team members. Imagine you are a team thrown together and briefed to get from one side of a river to the other. You have two plastic barrels, wooden planks and rope to assist you in getting across the river. If you do not examine the equipment and see what it may be able to do, you will never know how it can help you. It may be that it is of no use at all. You should also find out if anyone in the team has been in this position before. If so, they may have a solution that they prepared earlier!

Seek the Objective – After analysing the team situation it is very important that each member understands what the team is trying to achieve. If any member does not understand what the overall objective is, that person is a threat to the success of the task. There must be team harmony and a clearly understood objective.

Strategy Options – Decide 'how' the team is going to achieve the objective. Everyone should take part in this process and come up with ideas on how the objective can be met. It is possible that a number of different approaches to completing the task will come out of the discussion. This is what is required, the more ideas you have the stronger the final solution will be.

Analyse the Options – Take a look at the different ideas that have come out of the team discussion and decide which one will be the best for completing the task.

Decision – The members of the team must agree which option will provide the best solution for completing the task. When it is agreed everyone must be happy with the decision that is made. Not everyone must agree that it is the best strategy but there must be a consensus. Everyone must be prepared to do what has been agreed. A dissenter will be a liability and become a burden to the team.

When this process has been completed the team are able to begin a series of actions towards completing the task. This is where you look at the things that you did, the problems that had to be solved and the interpersonal difficulties that were experienced. You must describe the interactions with your team colleagues that demonstrate the positive traits in the competencies.

Summary

Do not be tricked into thinking that detailed study of the core competencies is unnecessary. Like all jobs that you may have applied for in the past a 'Job Description' and a 'Skills Profile' will accompany an application. This is made available so that you are aware of what the job is about and the type of person the employer is looking for. The police service is no exception and the nature of the job and cost of training makes it essential to get the right person first time. Use the competencies to evaluate your strengths and weaknesses and then make sure you prepare yourself well for the assessment.

Chapter 5

Matching Yourself to the Core Competencies

The Assessment Centre exercises are designed to test `What` and `How` you do things in particular circumstances. It follows that you need to know what and how you do things before you go to the assessment. If you do not, then you must work this out before you get there. As with all interviews and tests you should be self aware and understand your strengths and weaknesses; this will enable you to present yourself in a positive light. That is what an employer is looking for and you have to provide it. Without this you cannot expect to pass the selection process.

As a preliminary to any test of your suitability for a job it makes sense to look very carefully at the skills required for the job and check whether you match them or not. By way of illustration, there is little point applying for a job that requires a university degree in mathematics if you do not even have a General Certificate of Secondary Education (GCSE) in the subject.

How to Prepare

As outlined in chapter 4, there are seven core competencies that have been determined as essential skills for the role of police constable and you will be tested against all of these during the assessment process. To make sure you are fully prepared you should undertake the following preparatory work on the competencies:

Know and understand the **seven** defined core competencies.

And in each one:

- Understand the **Level Required** (standard)
- Examine the **Positive Indicators** (behaviours)
- Recognise the **Negative Indicators** (behaviours)

When you have done this you will need to think of an example from your life experience that demonstrates the competency. This is often not an easy task. The best way to tackle this is to think of an experience you have had and then work back towards the competency. The following example of team working demonstrates the process.

Example: Team Working

Firstly...

You are able to recall a time when... '*I had to organise a competitive team hike across the Brecon Beacons in Wales. It was particularly hazardous for the competitors and organisation of the event required a team of 10 people. There was a whole raft of different things to be completed to ensure the smooth and safe running of the event, including a close relationship with the emergency services in the event that anything went wrong...*'

Secondly...

Examine the **Positive Indicators** under the required level and try to find evidence of as many of them as you can from the team task you had to complete. You may, for example, be able to find enough to demonstrate the following:

- Understand your own role in a team
- Make time to get to know people
- Offer help to other people
- Develop mutual trust and confidence in others
- Willingly takes on unpopular tasks
- Contribute to team objectives
- Acknowledge there is often a need to be in more than one team

Thirdly...

Check that you do not display any **Negative Indicators.** You should not display any negative indicators as these will suggest to the assessors that you do not possess the necessary skill.

Fourthly...

Look at the **Required Level** and see if the skills you have displayed reach the standard:

'Works effectively as a team member and helps build relationships within it. Actively helps and supports others to achieve team goals'

If you do, you have just identified your skills in that area and become more self-aware.

Repeat this for all the competencies and you will then have a good understanding of each competency and what skills you have in that area. You will then have 'matched' yourself against the skills required to become a police officer through exposing the areas where you have particular strengths and those where there is scope for development.

Having trouble matching yourself?

For many candidates, this may not appear as simple as it seems. It is sometimes difficult to think of specific examples of behaviours. This difficulty is often experienced when completing the Application Form and when answering the questions in the Competency Based Interview.

If you are finding the matching process difficult and you are unable to come up with an example of your behaviour under a particular competency, try the following approach. For the purposes of illustration consider the competency Problem Solving.

1. Take a close look at the **Required Level**. You will notice that it talks about:

- Gathering enough information to understand the specific issues and events
- Uses information to identify problems and draw logical conclusions
- Makes good decisions

2. Look at the **Positive Indicators**. You will see that some of them give you a clue as to what is required:

- Identifies where to get information and gets it
- Separates relevant information from irrelevant information
- Identifies and links causes and effects
- Takes a systematic approach to solving problems
- Makes good decisions that take account of all relevant factors

They clearly indicate that you have to gather information to help identify the cause of the problem and then take a systematic approach to solving it.

3. By contrast, if you look at the **Negative Indicators** they will tell you what behaviours you should <u>not</u> exhibit!

4. Now consider the simple problem solving model SARA (outlined in chapter 4) to give you a structure on which to build the information you have read about the competency:

<u>S</u>earching - When you perceive you have a problem it is important that you look at it carefully, from all angles, to confirm this is an issue that needs resolving.

<u>A</u>nalysing – when you have confirmed there is a problem it is important to analyse it to establish the root causes. You must dig deep into the problem by examining information, documents, speaking to people and looking at the knock-on effects and how it impacts on other systems and processes.

<u>R</u>esponding – this is about making an informed decision about what is to be done to resolve the problem and putting in place measures and changes to deal with the issues. The actions you take should deal with the causes of the problem rather than just treating the symptoms.

<u>A</u>ssessing – after the measures have been put in place it is important to check that the decisions that have been made to deal with the issues were effective.

Follow up checks must be made to ensure the causes of the problem have been eliminated.

You should now be in a position where you understand what is required and all you have to do is think of an occasion when you solved a problem in this way. Once you have the example break it down into the elements they are looking for in the definition of the competency.

If you are still finding this difficult, a good tip is to make sure you avoid dismissing an example because you feel it does not seem dynamic or glamorous enough. Sometimes, it is the simple examples which are the best and can be structured for a very effective delivery. Also, talk to friends and colleagues to help you identify examples.

Summary

By the time you have matched yourself to all seven competencies you will have a good understanding of each one and you will be confident you have discovered your strengths and weaknesses. By examining the examples quoted in chapter 2 and in chapter 6 you will see how episodes from your life experience can be used to demonstrate your skills. The matching process is the first step in preparing yourself for completion of the Application Form and attending the Assessment Centre.

Chapter 6

Competency Based Interview

The Competency Based Interview is designed, as with the other exercises, to test the level of skill that you have in particular competencies. You may have envisaged attending an interview where you find yourself sitting in front of two or three panel members who will question you in turn about a range of matters related to your experiences of life and suitability for the job. This is not the kind of interview you will undertake at the Assessment Centre.

When you enter the interview room you will find a single assessor sitting at a table. They will ask you to sit down and then commence briefing you about the procedure. Do not expect all of the pleasantries you might get at the traditional interview because the Competency Based Interview is structured and the same for everyone. The assessor will explain that the interview will last for 20 minutes and you will be required to answer 4 questions. You will have 5 minutes allocated to each answer. There will be an opportunity to read the question from a card to clarify what is being asked.

The interviewer will draw your attention to this at the appropriate time.

The core competencies that you will be asked questions about are subject to change from time to time but you can expect a mix of four competencies, for example, you may have to answer questions on:

- Respect for Race and Diversity
- Team working
- Community and Customer Focus
- Personal Responsibility

In addition, your ability in Effective Communication will be judged during the course of answering the questions. It goes without saying that you should speak clearly, do not use slang, do not repeat yourself or speak in a boring monotone way. Being cheerful and enthusiastic goes a long way to scoring good marks.

You should expect a typical question to look like the following example in the Respect for Race and Diversity competency:

'Please tell me about a time when you experienced a clash between someone's view on an issue and your own strongly held views'

You will then respond with your answer to the question.

Your preparation for the exercise should enable you to speak for about 5 minutes. However, this may be difficult to judge and deliver on the day. Do not worry if you think you will speak for a shorter period or if you are likely to overrun.

The assessor will guide and help you. If you cut the answer short or dry up the assessor will put 'probing' questions to you and get your started again. They may ask questions like:

- What did you do?
- Why did you do that?
- What happened?
- What factors did you take into account?
- Is there anything else you wish to say?

If you finish your answer before the end of the allotted 5 minutes the assessor may say,

'We will now move on to the next question'

If you speak for longer than the allotted 5 minutes the assessor may say,

'I must stop you there, we will now move on to the next question.'

At the end of the interview you will leave the room.

It is important to recognise that the assessor is highly trained and has a job to do.

They must operate professionally, objectively and dispassionately. You will not get any indication of how well or badly you have performed because the assessor will be focussed on listening very carefully to your answers and completing a marking sheet; so do not look for lots of smiles and eye contact because you may not get it.

In many respects this is an alien environment, so do not be surprised if the whole experience is detached and mechanical. It is the same for everyone and is designed to be fair.

How to Prepare

Your preparation for this exercise will have already begun when you read and understood the core competencies for the role of police constable in chapter 4. If you then followed up with the matching process described in chapter 5 you will be in a position to develop your responses to the questions. The guiding principles for your preparation require that you must:

- understand each of the competencies you will be asked questions about
- articulate an example that demonstrates the competency effectively
- use your example to respond to the question asked

To do this you must choose a real life experience that you can talk about comfortably for five minutes.

This means that you should have sufficient information to talk about and you are happy talking about the subject. If the example is of a personal nature and you might feel embarrassed about telling the assessor, consider whether you wish to use it or think of something more comfortable to deliver.

It is possible that after the matching exercise you have a number of examples but they only run to a paragraph and you are wondering how you can speak about them for 5 minutes. Do not worry and do not dismiss them. After following the proposed structuring process below you may soon find you have more to say than you first realised.

Structuring your Answers

Think of each answer as a short speech or presentation during which you will tell a story about something you have done in your life that will demonstrate the positive indicators contained in the competency. The only way to do this is to have a structured approach to your delivery. This does not require a complex project plan; it can be a simple structure that reminds you there must be an 'Introduction', a 'Narrative' and a 'Conclusion'. This enables you to introduce your example, then move into the narrative, making the key points along the way and then conclude things by checking that you have answered the question.

This can be simply illustrated using the Team Working competency. We know from a close examination of the core competencies and the matching exercise that the required level in team working is, 'Works effectively as a team member and helps build relationships within it. Actively helps and supports others to achieve team goals'. Now look at the positive indicators and you will notice, amongst others, they include,

- 'Understands own role in a team'
- 'Actively takes part in team tasks in the work place'
- 'Co-operates with and supports others'
- 'Willingly takes on unpopular or routine tasks'
- 'Acknowledges that there is often a need to be a member of more than one team'

Use these, and the others listed, to build a framework of questions that prompt you to tell a story that demonstrates each positive indicator. As you answer those questions you should be able to state 'what' you did and 'how' you did it. Here is an illustration of a simple plan for the competency Team Working. Assume the question is:

'Tell me about a time when you worked as part of a team?'

Introduction

What was the situation?
What was the problem?
How did the team come together?

Narrative

What was my role in the team?
How did the team deal with the issues?
Was I a member of more than one team?
Do I actively take part in team tasks?
Am I open and approachable?
Do I get on with people?
Will I accept help?
Do I help others?
Do I trust people, do they trust me?
Will I do unpopular tasks?
Do I focus on team objectives?

Conclusion

Have I answered the question?
What was the outcome?
How was it perceived?
What was the knock-on effect?

You should now have drawn out a whole range of different pieces of information from your example that demonstrate your team working behaviours. You can now plan your answer on paper and sequence the events in chronological order. In the narrative section it is useful to break down the sequence of events into three or four key points to help you remember and organise your thoughts.

1. Introduction

2. Narrative
Key point (a).........
Key point (b).........
Key point (c).........
Key point (d).........

3. Conclusion

If you are finding this difficult you should consider asking family, friends and work colleagues what they think about your team working behaviours. Ask them the same questions you have listed in your plan and see what they come up with. This will help you build a picture of yourself.

The DVD that accompanies this book demonstrates the application of this approach in delivering the answers to the questions. (See Appendix 6)

What follows are three typical scenarios that might be the result of a matching exercise and that can be used as a basis to develop answers for the interview.

Examples:

1. Respect for Race and Diversity

'When I was working as a civilian custody officer in the police station cells a prisoner told me he was a Muslim and needed to pray. I was aware that we had no facilities in the cells for him to pray. I asked him what his requirements were. He informed me that he needed a 'clean' cell – one without a toilet. I moved him to a clean cell and asked what else he needed. He needed a mat to kneel on so I gave him a clean towel.

He also wanted to know which direction was east. I got a compass and indicated the direction for him. He was most appreciative of what I had done for him.'

2. Team Working

'I was on an outward bound course in Wales. At one stage we had to carry out a team exercise in a group of six which involved reading maps and compasses to cross a part of the Brecon Beacons. Things were fine until one of the team twisted an ankle. This created a major problem because we had a long way to go and the weather deteriorated and darkness was coming down. We had to work as a team analysing the situation we found ourselves in and coming up with the best solution. Of course, everyone had different ideas and it was important to let everyone have their

say. Nevertheless, we had to come to a solution. We discovered we all had different skills that were important to this situation. We finally came to a consensus decision and agreed a course of action. We survived and we realised how important it was to get on and work together. My role was to keep everyone on track – like a manager would.'

3. Problem Solving

'I was responsible for the production of a chemical for use in farming. The chemical was prepared on a production line with ten different processes. The product was tested regularly for defects. On one occasion there was found to be chemical imbalance according to the product specification. It was not possible to identify where the problem was in the process by carrying out a simple test.

I set about gathering information to identify the problem. This required separate chemical analysis of each of the chemical processes in the ten preparation stations, examining the logged information and interviewing each of the staff engaged in the process at each station. Through systematic analysis it was possible to identify where the problem was.

It transpired from investigation that the % of chemicals had been put together in incorrect volumes at one of the stations.

When the operative was questioned it was revealed that he had been incorrectly trained in the preparation process. As a result of what was discovered it was possible for me to write a report outlining the problem, have the operative re-trained and the training course amended for the future. Subsequent assessment, after adjustment, proved that the problem had been eradicated and the product specification was achieved.'

Summary

The Competency Based Interview is often perceived by candidates to be the most difficult of all the exercises you will have to undertake. In reality, this is the easiest of them all and a great opportunity to score some good marks. The greatest difficulty is finding examples from your life experience. Once you have overcome that problem and thought of an example, even if you only have the seed of an idea, when you have developed it you may find there is more than five minutes worth of material and it will have to be trimmed down. So, do not panic, remain calm about this exercise. Use friends, relatives and work colleagues to help you come up with ideas. Often other people have a clearer view of what you have done and achieved than you do yourself. When asked they will often say, "What about the time when you were involved in...?", and there is the exact scenario you were looking for!

Chapter 7

Interactive Scenarios

The Interactive Scenarios are designed to assess your ability to deal with people. The role of a police constable is largely about people and their problems; therefore, this is a very effective way of assessing your skills and potential for development in this area. Police officers frequently deal with people who are emotionally unstable, drunk, angry, defiant and unhelpful. Often, they have to be arrested as well. However, the scenarios are not police based and they will not be violent or argumentative confrontations. In fact, time is limited; each scenario exercise only lasts for 5 minutes and is designed to enable you to demonstrate your skills. So do not fall into the trap of believing you are going to spend the whole time subduing a violent or aggressive person.

You will be in role as a newly appointed Customer Services Officer at the Westshire Centre and part of your role will require you to deal with complaints and problems that staff, customers and visitors bring to you. It is, as the job title suggests, a typical problem solving role. You will have to demonstrate a structured approach to dealing with the person showing that you are in control. Also, you must show that you are sensitised to their needs, give them empathy and provide a solution to their problem or complaint. The process is designed to provide you with opportunities to do and say the right things so that you can score well in the competency areas that will be tested. The role actors and assessors are highly trained and experienced; they are there to enable you to give your best.

It is important that you enter into the spirit of the exercise and prepare yourself well prior to arriving at the Assessment Centre. You must 'become' the newly appointed Customer Services Officer at the Westshire Centre for the day. You must be fully aware of your role, the key features of the Centre and the policies that affect how you do your work. Many candidates find it difficult to get into role.

Naturally, if you turn up on the day without preparation, it will be difficult, but if you have read The Westshire Centre Welcome Pack, and rehearsed it thoroughly, it will help you respond intuitively to the issues presented. You should also try and be yourself. Of course, this is easy to say but is difficult to do in the context of an Assessment Centre! However, you should try to deal with the role actor as a human being who has genuine concerns, requires some understanding and is looking to you for help. So, smile, show concern and be genuine!

Process

You will be required to deal with four interactive scenarios where a role actor and an assessor will be present. Each scenario is divided into a Preparation Phase and an Activity Phase.

In the **Preparation Phase** you will be allocated to a room where you will be provided with written information that may consist of letters, reports, policies, plans or a mix of these. You will be allocated 5 minutes to read the information and, if you wish, make rough notes. At the end of the 5 minutes a buzzer will sound and you should leave the room, taking any notes you have made with you, and enter the Activity Phase room nearby.

In the **Activity Phase** you will find a role actor and an assessor. You will then be in role as a newly appointed Customer Services Officer and you must interact with the role actor and deal with issues as they arise. The assessor will make notes during your performance. After 5 minutes has elapsed a buzzer will sound and you should leave the room and return to a preparation room.

This process will be repeated four times and when all of the four scenarios are completed the exercise will end.

Competencies

The Interactive Scenarios are designed to test whether you currently have the competencies and future potential to become an efficient and effective police officer.

The assessor, in each of the scenarios, will be looking for the required level of skills and will include all, or a mix, of the competencies:

- Community and Customer Focus
- Effective Communication
- Personal Responsibility
- Problem Solving
- Resilience
- Respect for Race and Diversity
- Team working

How to deal with the Interactive Scenarios

Each interactive scenario tests different aspects of the skills identified in the core competencies. It is, therefore, important that you adopt a structured approach to dealing with each role actor. In this way, you will be able to present your skills to the assessors in the most impactive and effective way. The following model simplifies the approach you should adopt in the Preparation and Activity Phases:

1. Preparation Phase

When you enter the room try to relax and do not rush. You will have 5 minutes to read the briefing material in preparation for the scenario. You can make notes on rough paper that you can take with you into the activity room. After you have read the material ask yourself three questions:

> **'Do I understand the information?'**
>
> **'Do I know what I have to do?'**
>
> **'Do I know who I am going to speak to?'**

If not, read it again.

2. Activity Phase

As you enter the activity room identify the role actor (this will be obvious), make eye contact and follow the **'seven point plan'**:

- **Introduction** - say 'hello', introduce yourself, shake their hand and tell them about your role and what you do in relation to complaints and problems presented by staff and members of the public.

- **Reassurance** – reassure them that you will listen carefully to what they say, deal with the issues they raise and that you intend to reach a satisfactory conclusion by the end of the session. Give them the confidence that you are in control and you can make things happen.

- **Get the Facts** – ask them what the problem is and get them to tell you what happened or tell them how you see the facts.

- **Check the Facts** - ask probing questions and gather as much detailed information as possible from them. Get to the root of the problem so you know what you are dealing with.

- **Consider the Options** – what is the best course of action in this case or what can you do to solve the problem. Tell them what you intend to do to reach a satisfactory outcome. Check if they are satisfied with the outcome.

- **Make a Decision** – be resolute in making a decision about your intended course of action or what you are going to do.

- **Reassurance** – reassure them that you will deal with issues raised and try to prevent this happening again in the future. Also, if they have any future problems to come back and see you right away.

Throughout you must show empathy, be pleasant, show interest, give a service, be concerned and be positive.

The **'seven point plan'** is a typical customer service 'approach' and is not designed to be definitive in the sense that it will fit all scenarios perfectly. It will be necessary to be flexible and adapt it to deal with different situations. It has proved to be highly effective in organising an approach to each scenario providing a start point, an interactive process and a finish point. If you learn and understand the model you can apply it intuitively and then concentrate on dealing with the details of the scenario and demonstrating the competencies.

The DVD that accompanies this book demonstrates the application of the seven point plan in a scenario at a Local Authority car park ticket office where a lady complains about receiving a parking ticket from an attendant who was rude to her. (See Appendix 6)

Here are some examples of the problems you may have to deal with during an interactive scenario:

The Drop Inn Coffee Shop

HiFi Electrics is having a massive advertising campaign for electrical goods. They have flat screen televisions, hifi systems, digital radios and many other lines blaring out noise to draw attention to their products. They have all the store front doors open to draw customer's attention.

The Drop Inn Coffee Shop next door to HiFi Electrics is a charity meeting place for senior citizens. The visitors to the coffee shop are finding it difficult to carry on a conversation and finding the noise excessive. They are finding it difficult to carry on their normal business because of the disruption being caused.

The manager of the coffee shop has complained to the manager of HiFi Electrics who has refused to turn the sound down. In fact, the two managers are now in dispute and not talking to each other.

The coffee shop manager has asked to see you and wants you to resolve the situation.

Cleaning Staff

Sally, a female member of staff on the cleaning staff, is upset and wishes to speak to you about another member of staff.

She complains that a new young male member of staff who is working with her cleaning in the maintenance department has been making unwelcome suggestive comments and touching her. In fact, these amount to sexual harassment as he has touched her leg on several occasions, talked lewdly about her body and suggested he would like to have a 'romp' with her.

You have to deal with her complaint.

Summary

It is essential that you prepare very carefully for the Interactive Scenarios because they are a vital element in the assessment process and they can prove to be intimidating for many people. If you have been involved in customer service work you will have some experience of dealing with people who have problems, but you should not be complacent. The Interactive Scenarios test all of the competencies apart from the written element of Effective Communication so you will have to think deeply about how you demonstrate your skills. The seven point plan is the starting point for your preparation. It is important to have a clear structure to help you through the scenario so that you can obtain as much information and make effective decisions about solutions to the problem.

Chapter 8

Written Exercises

The role of a police officer, as you will be aware, involves a considerable amount of paperwork. The vast majority of the paperwork is concerned with the investigation of crime and the preparation of case papers for court proceedings. Statements from witnesses and reports seeking advice or summarising cases are typical requirements of an investigation and the follow up processes. As with any organisation there is a vast quantity of internal communication by way of reports and with people outside the organisation by letter.

E-mail and text has superseded many of the hard copy reports and letters but this does not mean the formality of written communication should be lost. It is important to your integrity and that of the police service that you communicate effectively and professionally. The police service, therefore, requires a good standard of written English in the compilation of letters and reports.

The Assessment Centre requires you to demonstrate the required skill to a minimum standard. You must achieve a score of 44% to pass the written communication standard. Even if you achieve the pass mark for your overall performance in the exercises, you will fail if you do not achieve the minimum requirement in the competency Written Communication.

Process

The National Recruitment Model (NRM) requires Assessment Centre candidates to undertake two 20 minute Written Exercises. Since the NRM was introduced the NPIA have used a letter and a report in these exercises. More recently, two proposal reports have been used. The NPIA are obviously at liberty to change this in future years. But they will make clear what is required in the information they provide you before the assessment and that given during a briefing on the day.

However, before you get to the Assessment Centre you should know the difference between a letter and a report and be able to draft each one. You also need to understand that the exercises are designed to test whether you can communicate formally using well constructed and well presented written English. The modern usage of e-mail and text often demonstrates a very casual approach to communication skills that includes abbreviation, poor spelling, lower case and a general demise of the more formal approaches of the past. This will not be acceptable to the police service.

As in the case of the Interactive Scenarios, you will be in role as a newly appointed Customer Services Officer. You must be aware of your role and the key features of the Westshire Centre, including policies and procedures that might be applicable to the problems you will have to deal with. If you prepare well before you attend the centre you should have no difficulty assimilating the problem and preparing your response to it.

Each of the Written Exercises will last for 20 minutes. Pens, a proposal template and paper for rough work will be provided. You will be fully briefed by an assessor on what is required. You can make rough notes which will not be assessed. When you have 5 minutes and 1 minute remaining before the conclusion of the exercise you will be warned. The written work will be assessed after you have completed the Assessment Centre.

Competencies

In the Written Exercises you will be assessed against the core competency Effective Communication. This will be testing whether you can communicate ideas and information in writing, that you can use language and a style of communication that is appropriate to the situation and the person being addressed. You must also be able to make others understand what is going on. There is a particular emphasis on spelling, punctuation and grammar.

In addition, you will be assessed against other competencies to test your ability to demonstrate the sensitivities of dealing with people and their problems, the importance of recognising diversity, solving problems and using team working to facilitate the process, as well as taking responsibility and having a customer focus.

How to deal with the Written Exercises

In relation to both letter and report writing there are some general principles that you should adopt to ensure your approach to the composition is organised. These take the form of a structured approach to sorting your ideas, information and arguments before writing up the document. There are also some 'Do's' and 'Don'ts'. Always ensure you read the information you are given very carefully and be clear on the structure you are going to use before you begin writing.

1. Sorting Ideas

- Jot down ideas and ask yourself plenty of questions
- Look for a suitable structure for presentation e.g. 'for' and 'against'

- Sort the best material under paragraph headings and in logical sequence
- Provide 'links' between the paragraphs
- Remember that each paragraph is built on one main topic and should develop with illustrative detail

2. Do's and Don'ts

Do:
- Plan your structure on rough paper and decide on the best approach
- Keep to the subject and make your meaning clear
- Develop the theme for each paragraph and link them together
- Make your opening and concluding paragraphs as effective as possible
- Work out your sentences mentally before writing them
- Vary the length of your sentences
- Be prepared to rework parts to ensure they fit
- Read through to ensure it makes sense

Don't:
- Write what is too obvious or superficial
- Repeat yourself or ramble
- Use slang
- Write disconnected sentences or paragraphs
- Be pompous or condescending
- Use too many words where one would do

The Letter Layout

You must have a clear idea of what is required in a formal letter and you must practice the writing of a letter until you can do it intuitively without any detailed thought.

In the context of the Westshire Centre, and your role as the Customer Services Officer, you are likely to be required to respond to a written complaint from a customer.
There are many letter formats in use today, however, for the purposes of the Assessment Centre, it is recommended that a more traditional and simple approach is used.

The template below is self explanatory but you should note the following important points.

- In formal letters your address is positioned in the top right of the page followed by the date.

- It is customary to put the addressee name and address on the left side below the date.

- It is also very important to understand the rules for mode of address. If you do not know the addressee, use 'Dear Sir' and sign off the letter 'Yours faithfully'. If you know the addressee or you have previously written to them, use 'Dear Mr Blank' and sign off 'Yours sincerely'.

You should note that there is no capital letter for 'sincerely' or 'faithfully'.

The following template demonstrates what is required and is recommended as a basis for your formal letter.

Letter Template

(Your address)

....

....

....

WX2 6GY

(Date in full)   **22nd May 2006**

Customer Name & Address *(Addressee)*

Dear ....,

Acknowledgement...............................

Introductory Paragraph/Reassurance.......

Background Information

   Actions
   1............................
   2............................
   3............................

Concluding Paragraph..........................

Yours sincerely

..................................(Signature)
Designation (your role)

Example - Letter Writing Exercise

1. Your Role

You are the Bookings Manager for Blanktown Excursions and you are in receipt of a letter of complaint from a customer who has been on a coach trip to London. The customer has been on many trips in the past and never complained before.

2. Briefing Information

You have a copy of the itinerary of the London sight seeing trip and it details the start time as 9.30 am on Sunday and lists the expected times of visiting London Bridge, Houses of Parliament, Tower Bridge, St Paul's Cathedral and Covent Garden during the day. It also states that a hot three course lunch will be provided at 1 pm in the Topnotch Hotel, a tea consisting of sandwiches and a cream tea will be provided at Covent Garden Tea Rooms at 4.30 pm and the coach returns to the depot at 8 pm.

3. Letter of Complaint

Mr. Jim Giles,
32 Long Range Avenue,
Blanktown,
BT6 6HH

22nd March 2006

Dear Sir,

I went on the trip around London last Sunday. I have been on many trips before and have never complained.

However, this trip was not good. As I understood it we would be getting a hot three course meal at lunch time but when it was served the soup was cold and when we got the main course the meat and vegetables were also cold.

I complained to the waitress but nothing was done. When we stopped for tea in the afternoon we were served sandwiches and a cream tea. I was expecting a cooked tea.

On the way back home in the evening we pulled up outside a pub called the Three Pigeons in Blanktown and the bus driver asked if anyone wanted to go into the pub for a drink for half an hour. About ten people got off and were gone for a whole hour. This made the trip late back and I was not able to help my disabled mother get herself ready for bed. We didn't get back until 9.15 pm.

I don't like complaining but I am very unhappy about what happened and I would like you to tell me what you intend to do about it.

Yours truly,

Jim Giles

4. Your Task

Write a letter to Jim Giles dealing with his complaint.

5. Your Response

Bookings Manager
Blank Town Excursions
Blanktown.
WX2 6 GY

26th March 2006

Mr. Jim Giles
32 Long Range Avenue
Blanktown
BT6 6HH

Dear Mr. Giles,

Thank you for your letter dated 22nd March 2006.

As the Bookings Manager for Blanktown Excursions. I am responsible for dealing with complaints from our customers. I would like to reassure you that I will do all I can to deal with the issues you have raised to your satisfaction.
I would also like to ensure we can improve the

quality of service we provide in the future.

As I understand the position, you went on our sight-seeing tour of London last Sunday. Your lunch was cold when it was served, the afternoon tea was a cream tea when you expected a cooked meal and there was a stop at the Three Pigeons in Blanktown which made the trip late returning to the depot. I will deal with each of these complaints in turn.

Firstly, I will investigate why the lunch time meal you received at the Topnotch Hotel was cold and nothing was done when you complained about it.

I am committed to providing a high quality lunch for our customers and if this hotel cannot provide the standard we require then I will be seeking another supplier.

Secondly, I draw your attention to the itinerary for the trip. It does say that the afternoon tea would comprise of sandwiches and a cream tea. It may be that you inadvertently misread the itinerary before departure. However, I will be making the reference to the tea in bolder type in future to make it clear to customers what to expect.

Thirdly, the stop at the Three Pigeons was unscheduled. It was not within the remit of the coach driver to make a decision to stop at the public house, even if some of the customers requested the stop. Clearly, as in your case, it can inconvenience customers by returning late to the depot. I will be looking into this matter to see if there is a demand for a pub stop. If there is, it will be made clear on the itinerary and will not delay the return of the bus on time.

I apologise on behalf of Blanktown Excursions for the problems you encountered on the trip and to your Mother for any inconvenience caused. I will take the action I have referred to above. In addition, I would like to refund the cost of the trip and offer you a free trip of your choice. You are a regular customer and we value your custom and look forward to seeing you in the future. I would like to reassure you that should you have any suggestions that may improve our service or any further problems please do not hesitate to let me know.

Yours sincerely

Bookings Manager

The Report Layout

As with the letter, you must have a clear idea of what is required and you must be able to write a report without any detailed thought. A report is different to a letter. It is often an internal document and may be the product of researching information or a request for information by someone else in the organisation.

Often a senior manager will request a briefing report on something that has happened in the past or is to be held in the future to enable a complaint to be dealt with or to evaluate what occurred. It may also be the case that you wish to make a proposal report outlining how a future event could be managed effectively. Considerations such as health and safety, toilet facilities, security and marshalling could be relevant to the event.

Report Template

REPORT BY.............................

REPORT FOR...........................DATE............

PURPOSE OF REPORT...............................

Introductory Paragraph...................................

Background Information..................................

Diversity Considerations................................

Gathering Information................................

Using Information.....................................

Proposed Solution......................................

Concluding Paragraph...............................

..........................Designation

Example: Report Writing Exercise

1. Your Role

You are the Deputy Town Centre Manager for the Blanktown Town Centre. You have many responsibilities one of which includes preparing proposals for various events and activities for the information of the Town Centre Manager.

2. Briefing Information

The Town Centre Manager has sent you a memorandum stating that it is her intention to stage a charity fund raising event for a cancer charity in the Market Place on a Saturday afternoon in two months time. This will take the form of a 'Children's Extravaganza' with entertainment including comedians, dancing and drama on a stage in the middle of the Market Place and a number of volunteers collecting money for the charity.

The following information is known to you:

- The Children's Extravaganza is very popular and likely to attract vast numbers of young people.

- The event is on the same day that the local football team are playing at home.

- Football supporters always come through the Market Place to and from the match.

- The town centre will be at maximum capacity with shoppers as it normally is on a Saturday afternoon.

- There have been a number of crimes of handbag snatching recently on Saturday afternoons.

- Shop keepers always complain about events like this because of obstruction and noise when musical events are staged.

- A local transport initiative has helped disabled people from around the area to shop on Saturday afternoons alongside other shoppers. There are often a number of people using wheel chairs, those who are partially sighted and hard of hearing in the Town Centre.

3. Your Task

Write a proposal for the information of the Town Centre Manager about the organisation and security of the event. You have 20 minutes.

4. Your Response

REPORT BY..

REPORT FOR.............................DATE...............

PURPOSE OF REPORT......................................

I refer to your memorandum dated……..concerning the charity event featuring a Children's Extravaganza which is due to take place in the Market Place on…… This report outlines a proposal for the organisation of the event.

You should be aware that on Saturday afternoons the town centre has the weekly maximum of shoppers. Also, there is a football match that day and fans going to and from the match will move through Market Place. We also encourage wheelchair users and other disabled people into the town centre on Saturday afternoons. Recently, there have been a number of complaints about handbag snatches on Saturday afternoons and about noise and obstruction caused by previous events.

In line with our approach to diversity and our Equal Opportunity Policy it is essential there is no disruption to shoppers attending the town centre during the Extravaganza event, particularly the disabled, parents with children, older people and other minority groups. They must be able to go about their business uninterrupted. The demands of the event will be met but must be treated fairly and equally along side other town centre priorities.

My proposal for dealing with this event follows.

I will gather as much information as possible about this and previous events to identify any problems that occurred. I will speak to the event organisers, police, security, St. John's Ambulance, cleansing department, store representatives and licencees to assess the likely demands that will have to be met.

After evaluating the information I will call and facilitate a meeting of all the parties. I will then identify the key issues that need addressing and seek views from those present on how we can effectively deal with them.

At this stage, it seems appropriate that the event is controlled by stewards and barriers to facilitate entrance and exit. Blocked access to or danger to persons attending the Market Place must be prevented. We must ensure the St. John's Ambulance and other town centre facilities are sufficiently staffed to deal with the demands. The security staff and CCTV operators must provide a coordinated approach to the event. Also, stores and licensed premises must be vigilant and understand they are an integral part of the successful execution of the event.

The solutions will be contained within a written operational plan that will clearly identify what is required of all involved and provide contingencies for any unexpected problems.

I will take personal responsibility for gathering the information, facilitating the meeting and preparing the operational plan to ensure the smooth running of the event. It is essential to prevent any problems and ensure that all customers attending the Market Place have a pleasant and enjoyable experience.

....

Deputy Town Centre Manager

Summary

Do not underestimate the importance of preparation for the Written Tests. Experience has shown this can be the most difficult of all the exercises for some people. Even with a structured approach everyone will prepare a written communication in a different way. Written ability is similar to verbal ability in that it depends a lot on your learning, experience and usage. This means that intellectual ability in this area will vary from one person to another.

Whatever you think of your own written skills do not assume that these exercises will be easy. One of the major problems people experience is assimilating the information provided and then actually writing the proposal within 20 minutes. The secret to success is to adopt a structured approach and then practice writing a report in 20 minutes. Then get someone to read your script to check that it makes sense and your spelling, punctuation and grammar is good. To help you practice there are some exercises at Appendix 3.

Chapter 9

Numerical and Verbal Logical Reasoning Tests

It would be easy to assume that these two tests are simply designed to assess your ability in arithmetic and written comprehension. Obviously, like many professions, a police officer must have basic numerical skills and the ability to understand the written word. But there is more to these exercises; they are designed to test your ability to think logically as you use your numerical and verbal skills. It is significant that you will be assessed in these exercises against the core competency Problem Solving and Written Communication respectively. There is no minimum score to pass overall. You will be awarded a grade that reflects how many questions you get right.

An essential skill for a police officer is the ability to weigh up situations quickly and recognise what is required. So, you will be tested to assess your skills in the two areas and your ability to apply logical thinking to the problems that you are presented with. For example, the fact that you will have to complete 25 numerical questions in 12 minutes means that you have less than 30 seconds per question. That is a problem because you are under pressure. You will have to solve it using your numerical skills and logical thinking.

You must, therefore, prepare yourself on two fronts. Firstly, your basic numerical and comprehension skills will need to be honed. Secondly, you will have to develop your logical thinking to ensure you can make quick assessments and good decisions.

Numerical Test

This test consists of 25 arithmetic questions and you will have 12 minutes to complete them. Each question has 5 multiple choice answers. You will have to read the question, decide what the answer is and select the correct one from the five options. You then mark your choice on an answer sheet.

This is a typical example:

If one adult bus ticket costs £5.30, how much will it cost for a group of 13 adults?

A	B	C	D	E
£67.50	£68.90	£68.00	£58.90	£66.50

Answer...

When you decide what the correct answer is you will mark the answer sheet with your choice.

In this case the answer is B; therefore you will indicate this on the answer sheet.

You will find that the questions consist of fairly simple addition, subtraction, multiplication, division, fractions, percentages and area. The standard is within the reach of most candidates and it often only requires a brush up of your basic skills to feel comfortable with this test. Some may find it more daunting and will have to go back to basic principles.

How to Prepare

If you are finding the tests difficult it is advisable to refresh your skills by using one of the GCSE revision guides. These are very useful in explaining how to deal with the full range of calculations including fractions, percentage and area. Alternatively, you can contact your local tertiary college and enrol on a basic skills course that deals with numerical skills.

Once you have mastered the skills you should practice the timed tests frequently to maintain your skills to ensure you get a good mark on the day.

There are a number of tests at Appendix 1 to use in your practice sessions. You should

try to complete these in the allocated time of 12 minutes.

Technique

Obviously, you want to score the highest possible mark so you should think logically about how you are going to deal with this test. Most people would simply work their way through the questions dealing with each one in turn spending more time working out the difficult questions than the simpler ones. Unfortunately, you will not maximise your score if you adopt this approach because you will probably run out of time and leave a number of questions undone. Some of those may have been simple questions and you have not taken advantage of the opportunity to score maximum marks.

The best advice is to work quickly and carefully through all 25 questions answering those you can do with ease and leave undone those that are more difficult. You should then go back to the difficult questions and spend some time working them out. If you still have a number of questions unanswered with a minute to go you should make a calculated guess at the answer. This way you will not leave any questions unanswered. Remember, you will not get marks for questions that are left blank.

Verbal Logical Reasoning Test

This test consists of 31 questions that you will have to answer within 25 minutes. The test consists of six factually different scenarios each of which is presented as a short passage followed by bullet pointed known facts. There are 5 or 6 conclusions that you must evaluate to determine whether they are 'true', 'false' or 'impossible to say' in relation to the passage and known facts.

This is an example of what you may have to deal with:

The dead body of a man was found at 8 pm on wasteland adjacent to a petrol service station by a man walking his dog. The body had a knife embedded in the left breast. The police are dealing with the death as murder.

The following facts are known:

- *Cause of death was a knife wound to the heart*
- *The body was identified as Jim James*
- *A man with a knife was seen chasing Jim James at 7.50 pm*
- *Jim James and John Smith were arguing and swearing angrily at each other on the service station forecourt at 7.45 pm*
- *John Smith collected knives*

Conclusions:

1. *The man walking his dog killed Jim James (impossible to say)*
2. *Jim James died of natural causes (false)*

3. *A group of men were seen chasing Jim James at 7.50 pm (false)*
4. *The two men were sharing a joke on the forecourt (false)*
5. *John Smith may have stabbed Jim James (true)*

There are a number of tests at Appendix 2 to use in your practice sessions. You should try to complete these in the allocated time of 25 minutes.

How to Prepare

As with the numerical tests there is no substitute for practice. There is plenty of material that you can use to practice these tests and it should begin by understanding what is required and using a logical approach to make your deductions. It is very easy to 'read in' information by drawing on your experience of life to come to conclusions. By doing this you will distort the information contained in the passage and you will make assumptions that are wrong. It is most important that you evaluate the information given and you must not be tempted to introduce extraneous facts. The test is designed to see whether you can draw logical conclusions from the information provided.

Technique

It is important that you adopt a disciplined technique for dealing with these questions. This will help you avoid introducing other facts and distorting your thinking process. With each of the scenarios it is a good idea to first read the conclusions that you will have to make a decision about. By doing this you will know what you are looking for as you read the passage and the known facts. It is likely you will quickly spot the information you need to make a decision on whether it is 'True', 'False' or 'Impossible to say'.

This saves time by eliminating the number of times you will have to refer back to the passage.

It is also useful to recognise that the conclusions will either be 'closed' or 'open'. For example, 'John killed Jim' is a closed fact. There is no doubt from that statement that the person named killed the other. On the other hand, if the conclusion states that 'John <u>may</u> have killed Jim' this is an open statement and its veracity is questionable.

A logical approach to these closed and open conclusions will help you to make the right decision. It is a good idea to use a simple methodology to come to your answers.

'Closed' Conclusions – 'John killed Jim'

1. Look for some evidence that proves the conclusion. If the evidence is there to prove the conclusion it is 'True'. If there is no evidence to prove it is true move to step 2.

2. Look for evidence to disprove the conclusion. If the evidence is there to disprove the conclusion it is 'False'.

3. If there is no evidence to prove or disprove the statement it is 'Impossible to say'.

'Open Conclusions' – 'John <u>may</u> have killed Jim'

1. Look for some evidence that proves the conclusion. If the evidence is there to

2. prove the conclusion it is 'True'. If there is no evidence to prove it is true move to step 2.

3. Look for evidence to disprove the conclusion. If the evidence is there to disprove the conclusion it is 'False'.

4. If there is no direct evidence to prove or disprove the open statement do not assume it is 'Impossible to say'.

5. Look for circumstantial evidence that might lead to a *possibility* that the statement is true or false.

This is illustrated in the example given above. In the conclusion at 5, 'John Smith may have stabbed Jim James', although there is no direct evidence to prove or disprove the statement, it can reasonably be inferred that he 'may' have stabbed him by putting the circumstantial evidence together. The fact that he collected knives, was seen arguing with Jim James at 7.45 pm and a man with a knife was seen chasing Jim James at 7.50 pm is enough to assume that he 'may' have stabbed him. The statement is therefore true.

Summary

Do not assume that you will be able to do these tests easily and achieve a high grading. You may be disappointed with your overall mark for Written Communication if you do not prepare properly. Remember that Written Communication is only assessed three times.

Once in the Verbal Logical Reasoning Test and once in each of the two written proposals. As discussed in chapter 4, there is a compulsory pass mark of 44% in this competency and, therefore, you should take every opportunity to score well. As with all the exercises make sure you know you can score well because these will help you overcome the stress of the day and ensure a good overall performance.

Chapter 10

Interview Technique

Since the introduction of the National Recruitment Model a number of police forces across England and Wales have introduced additional selection components. This means, in addition to the NRM Stage 1 Application Form and Stage 2 Assessment Centre, some police forces hold selection interview panels. These panels may be held after you have passed the stage 1 application or after you have passed the stage 2 assessment. In each case, the police force is using the interview to decide whether you fit their local person specification for the role of constable.

The requirement to attend an interview of this type, before or after attending an NRM assessment, is purely a force decision based on their particular recruitment policy. Just as the pass mark varies from one force to another so can the requirement to attend an interview. In addition to the interview panel, some forces have introduced other elements like written and key board skill tests.

It is important that you recognise police forces may vary their selection components and you find out what will be required of you as you progress through the selection process. Contact your chosen force and ask them to be clear on what you will have to go through to be selected. A little clarity about the process will help you prepare mentally for success.

You should bear in mind that the interviews filter out around 10% of applicants. You must make sure you are not in that percentage group. If you do find yourself in that position it may be possible to transfer your application or assessment pass to another force but only if they are prepared to accept it.

Types of Interview

The type of interview you will have to undertake does vary from one force to another. Some have broad ranging interviews where you may be asked questions like, 'Who is the chief constable?', 'Should the police be routinely armed?', 'What is Neighbourhood Policing?' and 'Do you think cannabis should be legalised?'. Alternatively, you could attend a structured interview where you will have to answer set questions similar to those you can expect in the NRM Competency Based Interview like, 'Tell me about a time when you worked with others to achieve an objective?' (Team Working),

'Has there been a time when you had to show respect for another person's lifestyle?' (Respect for Race and Diversity) and 'Have you ever had to deal with an unsatisfied customer?' (Community and Customer Focus).

It is important that you find out what type of interview you will have to undertake. This will help with your preparation. In any event, you should undergo broad preparation for the interview and be prepared to answer questions in the following four categories:

Knowledge
'What do you know about...?'

Opinion
'What is your view on...?'

Logical thinking
'What would you do in the following situation...?'

Competency Based
'Can you give me an example of a time when you had to show resilience in the face of difficulty?'

How to Prepare

The Assessment Centre is designed to test your inherent skills against the seven core competencies. These will determine whether you fulfil the basic requirements to become a police officer and you will respond to appropriate training for the role. Although, to a certain extent, the assessment can discover your personality, it is primarily focused on skills.

For this reason, many police forces have introduced the interview panel. This type of interview is specifically designed to tease out your personality. The force wants to know whether you are the kind of person they want as a constable. Your personality and style can be important to the direction the force is going and the type of police work undertaken in the force area.

What is Personality?

The word 'personality' is derived from the Latin word 'persona' that was originally used to denote the different role masks used by actors in Greek plays. Over time the word came to mean the character being portrayed rather than the mask. The origins of the word are not so far from what some psychologists believe about personality today; that it is a series of assumed roles we act out in different situations.

Everyday we find ourselves describing and assessing the personalities of those around us. Whether we realise it or not, these daily assessments on how and why people behave as they do are similar to what personality psychologists do. While our informal assessments of personality tend to focus more on individuals, personality psychologists use broad personality styles that can be applied to different people. This has led to the development of a number of theories that help explain how and why certain personality traits develop.

Of course, this view raises the question of whether it is possible to measure a personality that is constantly changing in response to different situations. However, despite adapting our behaviour, we can see a consistency of behaviours across a range of situations and over time.

A simple definition of 'personality' is, *'a person's typical or preferred way of behaving, thinking and feeling'.*

This recognises that personality is affected by current circumstances and environment, but it is possible to identify enduring and stable characteristics. What creates those enduring characteristics is up for debate but it is clear that there is some clarity about factors that influence human personality. For example, age, genetics, family, education, life experience, environment and socio-cultural factors are all important in shaping a personality.

Discovering Yourself

Discovering yourself is the first step in the process of personal development. It needs to be structured and focused on the purpose of the development. Once the process of discovery is complete then a 'Personality Profile' will have been built and we can begin to prepare a development plan to enhance strengths and develop areas of potential weakness. Depending on the level of self-awareness, a development plan will be pursued over a defined period of time. It is important that the period of development is properly managed around a plan that includes discovery, input and reflection.

Before looking at the process of discovery it is important to understand what makes *you* who *you are*. Your personality is you and it is a combination of recognisable characteristics. It is made up of many components all of which you will need to discover. If others can recognise your personality it is extremely important that you recognise and understand it as well.

The Process of Self Discovery

This process is about using simple techniques to tease out the components of your personality. It is possible to break a personality down into as many dimensions (or slices) as you wish. But the more you use the more complex interpretation will become; it is important, therefore, to keep this as simple as possible.

There are a number of different methods of obtaining the information to discover personality.

(a) Psychometric Testing

Using a psychometric instrument is always a useful method of discovering things about personality. Providing it is objectively administered, the subject is honest and open, and the results are fed back to the subject in a constructive way, it will be a positive experience.

Many of these tests are focused on different personality traits and therefore it may be necessary to undergo a number of different tests to discover the various aspects of personality. A better practical approach is to use a test that is comprehensive.

After only one test many different aspects of personality can be drawn from it. The Saville and Holdsworth Occupational Personality Questionnaire (OPQ) is an example of a test that can provide a broad range of information.

The OPQ breaks down personality into 32 dimensions and provides a picture of personality, team working, leadership, reporting style, emotional intelligence, learning style, management competency and provides a range of development tools.

Whatever testing is used there may be a natural tendency toward cynicism about psychometrics and their accuracy. Accepting that our personalities are not an exact science then we should look on testing as just another tool to help us discover our personality profile. Experience shows that combining psychometrics with the other methods is a complimentary process.

(b) 360 Degree Appraisal

If there is any cynicism about psychometrics then the 360 degree appraisal is the ideal method of balancing perspectives. In this case a questionnaire structured around aspects of personality is issued to a number of work colleagues who are subordinate, contemporary and senior to the subject. The questionnaire is completed by the colleague who will indicate against each of the dimensions whether it is positive, satisfactory or an area for development. This is completed anonymously and returned to a moderator who will prepare a composite of the results.

This is a picture of how an individual is seen in the real world by a number of different people. If one person was to indicate that you do not listen when people are speaking to you, it is just possible that is indicative of a single bad experience. But, if all of the respondents indicate that you do not listen – then it is time to start listening.

This is a powerful tool and it is about how people see and experience you in the work place. You will soon begin to see a different person in the mirror each morning after going through this process. Subjects are often initially apprehensive about the process but find it rewarding and can aid the development process.

(c) Performance Development Review(PDR)

Annual Performance Review is an ideal tool to identify personality traits and professional skills. The PDR normally has a 'professional' section where performance is assessed against annual objectives. Although the evidence is provided by the appraisee for validation by the appraiser the process is largely one-dimensional in that there is still an element of 'top down' perspective.

Despite this the process is extremely useful in identifying personality.

(d) Work and Life Experiences

Throughout our lives we are constantly subject to experiences that challenge us and test the extent of our ability to deal with them. Sometimes these experiences are ideal examples of when we had to show leadership in a difficult situation or work in a team to get a job done within a very short time frame. These work and life experiences make up the rich picture of who we are and build the personality that we have. So, it is always a good idea to review these experiences and see what key personality traits came into play at that time.

(e) Special Experiences

These are the experiences we perhaps do not really want to have as part of our lives. You may have been involved in a traumatic incident like a car accident, a train crash or maybe you have had cancer or experienced the loss of someone close to you through a long and protracted illness.

For most of us these are the type of experiences that have a major impact on how we see the world. Sometimes these life changing experiences have a profound effect on how people lead their lives. It is possible something like this has touched you. Take some time to see how an incident of this kind may have impacted your personality and how your particular traits may have changed as a result.

Summary

These are just some of the methods of gathering information about your personality. The list is not exhaustive and you should be as inventive as possible in discovering yourself.

Areas for Discovery

Now that you have identified how to gather information about yourself, what kind of information do you need to know in relation to joining the police service? What follows is summary of the main areas should be familiar with.

1. Team Role

It is essential that you understand the work of Dr. R Meredith Belbin who published

'Management Teams - why they succeed or fail' in 1981. Driven by the increasing importance of team working in organisations at the time, Belbin set out to identify what made a good team, based on research in the UK and Australia. Although the book offered a number of important factors about team working, it is the team roles that became famous.

Belbin found that in successful teams eight roles could be seen in operation and concluded that, when selecting people for a team, filling the eight roles was as important as choosing technical skills or experiences. Belbin's ideas continue to be used by thousands of organisations because they make good sense and they work.

Today there are many different tools to identify individuals' preferred roles, and help teams to make the best use of each role. Although our preferred roles do not change over time, most of us can happily perform two or three of the roles, thus filling any gaps in the team's profile. That means that one person can cover more than one role - clearly important if you have a team of less than eight people!

The concept works best when used openly within a team or across an organisation. Individual preferences are only useful if they are known to others, so teams can assess who can best fulfil each role. You can use role identification as a form of team-building: it reinforces the fact that everyone is bringing something to the team and you all need each other if you are to be successful.

- **Plant**
  Imaginative, intelligent, source of original ideas.

- **Resource Investigator**
  Sales person, diplomat, resource seeker.

- **Chair**
  Sets team goals and defines roles.

- **Shaper**
  Task leaders who brings competitive drive.

- **Monitor Evaluator**
  Measured, dispassionate critical analysis.

- **Team Worker**
  Promotes team harmony, good listener.

- **Company Worker**
  Turns decisions and strategies into manageable tasks.

- **Completer Finisher**
  Worries about problems, checks details.

It follows, that awareness of our own preferred team role and others is a major contributor to understanding personal effectiveness in the work place, ensuring group cohesion and increasing overall organisational achievement. Police officers often work in teams and understanding your preferred role is important for practical purposes and for the Assessment Centre where the first of the positive indicators in Team Working is 'Knows own role in the team'.

2. Leadership Style

Whether you are on uniform patrol, managing a team at work, captaining your sports team or leading a major corporation, your leadership style is crucial to your success. Consciously, or subconsciously, you will no doubt use some of the leadership styles featured below, at least some of the time. Understanding these leadership styles and their impact can help you develop and adapt your style and to help you become a more effective leader.

A good leader will switch instinctively between styles according to the people and work they are dealing with. This is often referred to as "situational leadership". For example, the manager of a small factory trains new machine operatives using a bureaucratic style to ensure they know the procedures that achieve the right standards of product quality and workplace safety. The same manager may adopt a more participative style of leadership when working on production line improvement with his or her team of supervisors. Leadership comes in many guises and is a hotly debated subject. What constitutes this, sometimes elusive, commodity is often defined in different ways. For the sake of argument and simplicity the key principle of leadership is a clear vision of where you are going, the ability to communicate it and take people with you. *The Leadership Trust* describes leadership as:

**"Leadership is using your personal power
to win the hearts and minds of people
to achieve a common purpose"**

How you lead people to your vision is down to personal style. An analysis of leadership by Bass (1981) has identified five different preferred styles of leadership.

- **Directive Leader**
  Maintains responsibility for planning and control.
- **Delegative Leader**
  Minimal personal involvement.

- **Participative Leader**
  Favours consensus decision making.

- **Consultative Leader**
  Pays genuine attention to opinions and feeling of subordinates but maintains a clear sense of task objectives and makes final decisions.

- **Negotiative Leader**
  Makes deals with subordinates.

3. Reporting Style

This is about how we respond to and work for our managers. Different personalities prefer to respond to their manager in diverse ways. Some enjoy complete freedom to work autonomously without direct supervision and like to use their initiative to make decisions. At the other end of the spectrum, others may prefer to have opportunities to inject ideas into decision-making and be part of the process but is likely to accept decisions that go against their views.

It is possible to see the links with leadership styles in that a 'Self Reliant Report' is more likely to be a 'Directive Leader' than a 'Receptive Report'.

The styles are:

- **Receptive Report**
  Adheres to instructions and deadlines.

- **Self-Reliant Report**
  Prefers to work without restraints.

- **Collaborating Report**
  Many ideas to contribute.

- **Informative Report**
  Likes to be involved in decision making but accepts final decision, even if contrary to personally held views.

- **Reciprocating Report**
  Not afraid to speak up and undeterred by status.

4. Emotional Intelligence

Historically, innate intellectual ability was measured through an Intelligence Quotient (IQ). This measure of cognitive capacity typically uncovered intellectual agility in dealing with core academic subjects. Often IQ was used as a predictor of the level of expected academic achievement. It was also accepted that a 'high' or 'low' IQ was said to determine how successful you were likely to be in your working life.

Modern research evidence has questioned how accurate IQ is as a predictor of life success and modern neuroscience has suggested there is much more to it than intelligence levels. The 'Cerebral Cortex', the cognitive or thinking part of the brain, cannot work in isolation it requires the 'Sub Cortex', the emotional centre of the brain, to work with it. In effect, intellect and emotion are not mutually exclusive. They work together in a complimentary way to determine daily decision-making.

Emotional Intelligence (EI) is best described as:

"a type of social intelligence that involves the ability to monitor one's own and others' emotions, to discriminate among them, and to use the information to guide one's thinking and actions" (Mayer & Salovey 1995).

Simply put, one needs to be intellectually and emotionally aware to be successful in life. An imbalance or a lack of awareness is a waste of talent. It pays to know both your Intelligence (IQ) and Emotional Quotient (EQ), and get them to work together for you.

To assist in defining and understanding your EQ it is broken down, principally, into two dimensions.

Managing Feelings is how well you *manage* and *understand* your emotions and feelings.

Managing Relationships is about how well you *appreciate* the perspectives of others and how *flexible* is your style in adapting to different work and social situations.

The importance of EQ insight comes alive when the impact of emotional intelligence is applied to develop other skills like leadership, team working, individual performance, interpersonal exchanges, managing change and performance assessments.

For example, good leadership requires excellent self-awareness, self-control, awareness of others and social skills. Developing these EQ competences can have a major impact on personal effectiveness.

5. Learning Style

Learning is an individual experience. We all have a preferred style and it is well known that if a group of people with the same needs are given the same activity, some will learn a considerable amount whilst others will learn very little. This is because the activity will not suit all the learning styles of those within the group. It is possible, with reasonable accuracy, to predict individual learning styles through psychometric assessment to assist individuals understand and develop the most productive learning experiences. Styles fall into four common definitions.

Activist learns best from experiences which are new, competitive, exciting and high profile. They are people that thrive on learning 'on the job' and are not deterred by giving them a high profile.

Reflectors are people that enjoy learning from opportunities where they are able to stand back from events, watch, assimilate and think about what they are seeing before acting.

Theorist likes to have a model, system or theory into which they can link new concepts. A sense of order is preferred to probe basic concepts and assumptions.

Pragmatist learns best from activities that can be linked to the solving of problems or a real life opportunity in their job. Turning the subject matter into a practical reality helps them to learn more easily.

It is important for those who teach us to recognise the need for diverse learning opportunities to reach out and meet student needs. More importantly, in terms of personal development, it is imperative that we understand how, as individuals, we learn best. Without understanding our own preferred style we will not realise or maximise our true potential through the most appropriate and productive learning experiences.

6. Greatest Strength and Weakness

Strength – Make sure that you understand what particular aspect of your personality is your greatest strength. If you know what it is then you can use this as a base line from which you can support the development of others aspects of your personality and maximise your successes.

Weakness – We all have development areas that can weaken our performance. Recognising these is important. It does not matter what it is, providing you know how to manage it and turn it into a positive strength.

Often a great strength and a weakness can be the two sides of the same coin. For example, your great strength might be your strong vision and determination to achieve. This is very positive. But your strength will become a weakness if you are so enthusiastic that your drive and determination, particularly where your efforts are frustrated in any way, spill over into arrogance. Similarly, if you have bags of determination and drive but you fail to communicate your vision to your team and they do not understand what is required, your natural great strength, by default, will become you worst weakness.

An easy way in which to determine your strengths and weaknesses is through a 360 degree appraisal. Always be self-aware in these areas because you can frustrate many of your efforts to be successful purely through having a 'blind spot'. It is so important to your success that you are sensitised to your impact on other people.

7. Career Achievements

As a final step in the process of preparing a personal profile and a development plan, it is essential to assess what you have achieved in your career so far. What you have achieved so far is key to understanding the information gathered through the programme of discovery.

A good way of doing this is to gather information under four heads. Identifying the **skills** that you have developed during your working life helps to identify what you can do and what you are best at.

Recognising your **attitudes** to life, your work and the future will help to understand the cultural development you have gone through during your working life. This is useful in modelling styles for your future development plan.

Defining the **knowledge** that you have accrued through experiences to date helps in understanding whether you have a technical, strategic, commercial or other area of particular strength.

Underpinning these three broad areas is **experience**. Whatever your technical level of skills might be, without exposure to life and work experiences the natural process of continuous learning will not take place. The old adage that there is 'no substitute for experience' and 'you can't put an old head on young shoulders', has some truth. The secret is a subtle blend of all four of these areas.

Personality Profile

After having been through the process of discovery you should have a 'rich picture' of your personality. It is highly likely that you will have uncovered a vast range of skills, many of which are positive strengths and some where development will be of benefit. Either way you will have a much better appreciation of who you are and you should be able to pull together all of the various facets to build a 'Personality Profile'.

This will represent a box of jigsaw pieces that need to be sorted and grouped into areas where there are linkages. You will need to build these packages of skills into a cohesive framework that you can personally articulate.

Consider for one moment if you were asked the question, *'Tell me a little about yourself?'* would you be able to answer that question in a cogent and well structured way?

This information makes up your **Personality Profile** and is an introspective view of all your skills and abilities and where they match.

Using your Personality Profile

Now you are aware of these things about

yourself the trick is to use this information to best effect. This is about technique.

There is nothing magical about how you should approach the interview panel. It is a matter of going to the interview with a clear picture of what you want to tell them. You should be on a 'mission' of your own and should have formulated a personal strategy.

If you have completed your preparation, you will go the interview with a clear head and be on the offensive. There should never be a time when you go to an interview in fear of what might be said or done during the 45 minutes that you are in the room. If you are sitting in the chair in a defensive posture trying to fend off the questions, you are not going to be successful nor are you going to enjoy the experience.

If you imagine for one moment that you enter the interview room and the interviewer asks you the question, **'Why should we employ you as a police constable in this force?'** and gives you 45 minutes to answer the question. How would you feel? If you do not know where to start, you are not prepared for the interview. However, if you sit back confident in the knowledge that you have much to tell them and you have a well formulated personal strategy for delivering it, ***you are prepared***.

The reality is that the panel, in a broad ranging interview, will have questions that they will want to ask to elicit information about you in different categories. For example, they will want to know about your personal skills, professional skills, general knowledge and your ability to think logically in different situations. Accepting this is the case it is still possible to drive through your strategy and get across to the panel exactly what you want to tell them about why you should be selected. To do this you will need to set the agenda for the interview.

Setting the Agenda

Assuming that you have a good picture of your personality profile, it is a good idea to begin preparing your agenda by using the frequently asked first question designed as an ice breaker to get you going at the start of the interview, 'Tell us a little about yourself?'. In fact, it really does not matter what they ask you. If you were asked, 'Why should we select you to become a constable in this force?' it is really the same answer. In any case, if you have a well prepared agenda you will be nimble enough to deal with the slightly different inflexion in the response to a question.

With that in mind consider the question, **'Tell us a little about yourself?'**

It is most important that you structure a short response under three heads:

Past – Where you were born and brought up, what kind of education you received and how successful were you were academically is always a good point to start. Your parents and the type of upbringing you had can be very important. If, for example, if you moved 26 times before you were 18 years of age because your father was in the services, and you lived in various places across the world, could be a point that you can make about your natural resilience for change and dealing with different peoples and cultures. Similarly, if you were brought up in care then your experiences may be important to the personality that you are. You may also wish to mention your early working experiences.

Working Life – There is no sense in repeating your career record - times, dates and places - because they will already know that. This is your big opportunity to demonstrate what challenges, experiences and development opportunities you have had. This is where **you** set the agenda.

You should mention different situations you have been involved in at different times in your working life and 'throw down the markers'. For example, 'When I was working at 'Blank Town' I was an engineer working on the building of the new Orbital Road. This really tested my 'team working skills' and, 'When I was working in the city as a PCSO I had to deal with a clash between the two local ethnic groups. I had to show real problem solving skills and had to have a community and customer focus'.

The reality is that as you provide career highlights you are throwing down the 'markers' – things which highlight the competencies they are testing you against and your particular style of working. These will be things that you want them to ask you questions about because you can expand on them and they demonstrate graphically how you dealt with the situation. It will also demonstrate the skills required in that particular competency area.

The following diagram illustrates this approach.

The great thing is that the panel will be keen to explore some of the points that you have made because they are seeking to test those skill areas. This is about bringing the game to them rather than sitting back and them bringing it to you. By doing this you can tell them a little about you and throw down the markers knowing that they will want to explore them further. Even if the questions are not predictable, you will have a prepared script. It is an insurance policy to keep you on track.

This takes some practice but you will find that you will be able to 'snake' your way through the interview moving from one question to another by opening up another avenue of questioning and moving the interview in the direction that you want it to go – '...of course, this situation involving team working was very similar to the time when I had to demonstrate strong leadership at...'

Obviously, the panel members will have certain areas they wish to probe but you may find that because you have an agenda you will move from one area to another and cover the questions that they wish to cover.

With practice, you can anticipate the direction they want to go. You will know whether you are succeeding when one member hands over to another and states, 'I was going to ask you four questions but you seem to have answered some of those already, so I only have one question to ask'.

Future – To conclude your short agenda setting answer it is important to state where you see you career going over the next 5 and 10 years. It is always good to demonstrate, as you just have, that your career has so far been a progressive development process and you have every intention of moving it forward in the same way.

Answering Questions

After you have 'warmed-up' and set your agenda the panel will want to ask you questions. Normally, where there is a panel of two or three interviewers, the questions will be generically grouped and each interviewer will focus on the allocated area. It may be that they will want to ask questions about your knowledge of the force, why you want to join the police, force strategy, personal skills, dealing with scenarios, general policing knowledge and headline controversial issues. All of these will be linked to the competencies and will be delivered through 'closed' or 'open' questions.

Closed Questions

There are two definitions that are used to describe closed questions. A common definition is:

> *A closed question can be answered with either a single word or a short phrase.*

Thus 'How old are you?' and 'Where do you live?' are closed questions. A more limiting definition is:

> *A closed question can be answered*

with either 'yes' or 'no'.

Thus, 'Are you happy?' and 'Is that a cat I can see over there?' are closed questions, whilst 'How are you?' and even 'How old are you?' are not, by this definition, closed. This limited definition is also sometimes called a 'yes or no' question, for obvious reasons.

Using closed questions

Closed questions have the following characteristics:

- They give you *facts*.
- They are easy to answer.
- They are quick to answer.
- They keep control of the conversation with the questioner.

Open Questions

An open question can be defined as:

> *An open question is likely to receive a long answer.*

Although any question can receive a long answer, open questions deliberately seek longer answers and are the opposite of closed questions.

Using open questions

Open questions have the following characteristics:

- They ask the respondent to think and reflect.
- They will give you *opinions* and *feelings*.
- They hand control of the conversation to the respondent.
- Open questions begin with what, why, how, or describe.

Responding to open questions can be intimidating, as they seem to hand the baton of control over to the candidate.

However, a well-placed open question and plenty of preparation will leave you in control and enable you to develop your agenda. This then gives you the floor to talk about what you want and to draw the panel through intrigue or an incomplete story in the direction you want to go.

Open questions have become more common in recent years and are designed to give the candidate an opportunity to demonstrate the skills they have to offer. Your preparation will have included setting the agenda and in-depth study of different aspects of policing issues likely to affect the newly promoted officer. All that is required in this situation is to deliver a well thought out and structured answer.

The 'Thinking Box'

A structured delivery of your answer to any question is extremely important. An interviewer will want to hear an answer that demonstrates you have a good knowledge of the subject, that you have weighed up the arguments and come to a well reasoned conclusion, and personal viewpoint.

The only way to do this is to have carried out the necessary research into the topic and analysed it so that you can understand the positive and negative aspects of the arguments around the subject.

A good way of both studying the topic and delivering an answer on the topic is to use a simple structure like the 'Thinking Box'. This will help you to structure your thoughts around the topic supported by evidence. For example, how would you answer the following question:

'Should Cannabis be legalised?'

First of all, you will outline briefly what you know about the topic. Then you will present the arguments 'for' and 'against' the proposal to legalise Cannabis, and then draw some logical conclusions from the evidence. Finally, you will give your view. Never answer the question 'yes' or 'no'. You must argue the point to show what you know about the topic and that you have considered the arguments.

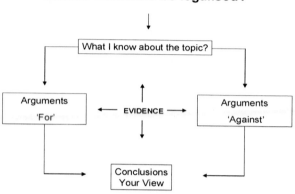

What I know about the topic?

- Social consequences of drugs are significant with mental health problems, addiction and death being a feature

- Crime is linked to drug habits and drug supply

- Cannabis is a category C drug

- Alcohol and tobacco are legal drugs and have many social consequences

- Cannabis is supposed to have medicinal properties – being investigated by the Government

- Strategy for tackling drugs is education, enforcement and treatment

Arguments 'Against'

- Legalising will raise the threshold of criminality – the lowest level of criminality will be raised
- More people will take cannabis because it is perceived safe – like alcohol and tobacco
- There will be more health problems - mental illness and death
- More strain on treatment of addicts
- Social impact considerable

Arguments 'For'

- Low level street crime connected with dealers would fade away
- The impure street drugs could be replaced by pure versions which will be safer
- Over the counter sales could fund research into the positive aspects of the drug
- Cannabis cultivation could be a viable commercial enterprise
- People who suffer from medical problems like Multiple Sclerosis (MS) and Arthritis could be given prescription cannabis to alleviate their symptoms

Conclusion/ Your View

In a sense, in questions like these, it does not matter too much what your conclusion and personal view is. Providing it is well reasoned and argued using a structured approach, it will come across as a well considered and thoughtful response to the question.

In this particular topic, you are safe in the knowledge that there are many different viewpoints amongst senior police officers, politicians and other commentators about the best way forward for dealing with cannabis. So far, none of them seems to have produced a solution to the problem.

Now think about topical issues and consider them using the 'Thinking Box' structured approach. For example, routine arming of all police officers, lowering the age of criminal responsibility and lowering the drink driving alcohol limit. This approach to your thought processes will broaden your knowledge of the topic and understanding of the issues.

Interview Behaviours

Researching Panel Members

As an essential part of your preparation it is a good idea to find out who the panel members will be and then research their backgrounds and experience. This will not necessarily give you an indication of the questions you will be asked but it will give you confidence knowing the pedigree of the person to whom you address your answer. In addition, the members of the panel are likely to be impressed if you have done your groundwork and know something about them.

Punctuality

Do make sure you know where the interview will be held. Make sure you know how to get there (by whatever means). If you go by car, you really need to research where you can park. Do not run out of petrol on the way. Leave home earlier than you need to on the day of the interview to deal with delays by traffic or for other reasons. When you get there be courteous to everyone you meet especially the Personal Assistant (PA) or Secretary receiving candidates.

Dress

You should dress smartly making special effort to make a good impression. Shoes should be shiny and hair well groomed. Men should wear a suit and tie. Women should wear a trouser suit with a high neck line. In both cases jewellery should be minimal. Do not wear anything new. Wear something that you are familiar with and you will find comfortable sitting in the interview for 45 minutes.

Hand Shaking

When you enter the interview room, never announce who you are and then move down the panel vigorously shaking their hands saying how nice it is to meet them and it is a pity the weather is so bad.

Remember, they know who you are and you should take your lead from the Chair of the panel. Wait to be invited to sit down and only shake hands if invited to do so by being offered a hand. If you are offered a handshake use a single hand and it should always be with an open, relaxed palm.

Sitting

When you are being interviewed, it is very important that you give out the right signals. You should always look attentive - so do not slouch in your chair. It is a good idea to sit into the back of the chair and consciously feel the chair running up your spine. This will prevent any tendency to lean forward. Keeping your head up will also help. If the chair has arms rest your elbows on them. Whatever you do make sure that you do not lean forward and be tempted to adopt the foetal position and end up looking at the panel from the level of the chair seat!

Hands

These are always a nuisance in formal interview situations because you never know where to put them. You should never fold your arms, nor should you sit on your hands. Most of us use our hands to assist with verbal communication so it is probably best to place your hands in front of you, palms down on your thighs and use them where you feel the need and return to that position. Entwining your fingers and breaking the knuckles and other nervous disorders should be avoided at all costs as they distract the interviewer and it may detract from the quality of your answers.

Legs

Like your hands, these are always a difficult item. You should never cross your legs as this can lead to slipping forward out of the chair and before you know it, you will be in the slouch position and have to pull yourself into the upright position. This is distracting. Also, do not cross your feet out in front of you or tuck them under the chair. This can lead to restricted blood flow and your legs or feet may become numb and lead to discomfort or, as a candidate once did, as he stood up to leave his leg collapsed and found himself looking up embarrassingly from the prone position on the floor.

Eye Contact

Always give the panel member that is asking you a question eye contact. This will help you to listen to the question and concentrate on what is being asked of you. Eye contact should not be slavish to the point that you stare at the panel.

It is always good to divert your eyes from direct contact as you think about the delivery of your answer after the question has been asked. Diverting your eyes slightly to the side or above the questioner enables you to maintain contact with the person and think clearly without feeling the pressure of the panel member is on you constantly.

Do not be tempted to look down at the floor, over your right shoulder or out of the window and watch the maintenance woman mowing the grass at the front of Headquarters. This will distract you and create the impression you are unprepared and desperately looking for inspiration.

As you answer a question you should not focus your eye contact solely on the questioner. Your eyes should look to the left and right to make contact with the other panel members. Make them feel that you are addressing the whole panel with your answer.

Also, never turn your back on panel members by shuffling around in the chair to face the questioner. It might make you feel less vulnerable but by obstructing their view of your torso they are less likely to trust you. This is a tribal thing. If you can see someone's head and torso, you can see the most vulnerable areas. This makes you want to trust them

Lying

Never lie to anyone in an interview, your body language and tone of voice or the words you use will probably give you away - classic body language giveaways include scratching your nose and not looking directly at the panel member when you are speaking to them.

Creating the right impression

It is important to create the right impression through facial expression. Smiles, non-verbal communication for listening and appropriate nodding for agreement and understanding are very important

Do's and Don'ts

- Don't leave your mobile phone or pager switched on.
- Don't chew gum.
- Try to avoid saying 'um' and 'er...'
- Do try to use correct grammar.
- Don't swear.
- Don't use slang.
- Don't smell of smoke, alcohol or strong deodorant.

Practice, Practice, Practice

Performing well in interviews is just like writing a good CV and covering letter - the more practice you get the better you will be. In addition, the more feedback you ask for, the more you can work on your technique in a constructive manner.

Chapter 11

General Advice and Guidance

If you have read this far it is fair to say you are beginning to wonder how you are going to assimilate all this information and where are you going to start. This chapter will help you to organise your preparation for the Assessment Centre by providing a structured approach to your development. This is a 'check list' or 'project plan' to provide a step by step learning guide that will ensure you do not miss anything that is important.

When To Start Your Preparation

Like any examination it is a good idea to begin your preparation with plenty of time to spare. It is no good spending a few sessions of study in the week leading up to your assessment day hoping that you will get through. Apart from failure, it does not show the level of commitment or the determination required to become a police officer.

The best approach is to speak to the recruiting department of your chosen force and find out how long an application will take to process before an appearance at the Assessment Centre. You should then work back from that date and give yourself a minimum of 3-4 months to complete your personal development plan.

This sounds like a long time. For some people this will be the case but others may need longer. We are all unique and our learning should be tailored to our personal learning style. Either way, learning is a gradual and cumulative process to develop the long term memory. Overnight cramming will only affect the short term memory and will not be consolidated.

Preliminaries

When you have made the decision to join the police service and you have gathered all your information together, it is a good idea to do some preliminary checks to make sure you will not be disappointed by rejection after you have put a lot of effort into the process. You should look at two areas in particular.

Medical Criteria

You will have to reach a number of medical standards that will include eyesight, hearing and body mass index (BMI). In addition, the police will wish to see a doctor's report from your general practitioner (GP). Most police forces seek medical information and put you through a medical examination by the police surgeon after you have passed the Assessment Centre. Clearly, you do not want something to be disclosed or discovered at this stage that will jeopardise your chances of getting through – especially after all the hard work you have put in.

The best thing to do is arrange to see your GP before you apply to discuss your intention of joining the police and see if there are any issues that may cause a problem. Knee and back injuries that have required invasive skeletal surgery are often a problem. If this is the case contact your chosen force and discuss it with them and see if it is likely to be a problem.

Entry Criteria

It is a good idea to examine each of the entry criteria to ensure you are eligible to enter the service. There is little point in carrying out all the hard work required to complete an application, submit it and then have it returned because you do not fit the criteria. That will waste your time and that of the force.

The criteria are to be found at Appendix 4. Read each one and make sure that you are eligible. For example, make sure you can demonstrate that you have been resident in the UK for 3 years or more to meet the residency rule. Also, check that you are not an undischarged bankrupt because that will be a problem. You will need to be discharged and provide a certificate to prove it.

When you are happy that you will meet these basic criteria and there will be no surprises ahead to catch you out, it is time to begin your preparation.

The Development Process

Stage 1 – Reading

Before you even consider putting pen to paper you should begin to read all the information and make sure you know what is required. Read the application form from cover to cover to ensure you know what to do. If there is any doubt read it again and refer to the 'Notes for Completion' at the back of the form. Also, read the NPIA documents 'Information to Candidates' and the 'Westshire Centre Welcome Pack' to get a clear picture of what will be required at the Assessment Centre. These latter two documents are normally sent to you 2-3 weeks before you attend the Assessment Centre but examples are available from the NPIA web site for down loading at any time. (www.npia.police.uk)

Stage 2 – Matching to Core Competencies

Examine the seven core competencies and carry out the matching process described in chapter 5. You should then have different examples of things that you have dealt with in your life under each of the skill areas. Remember it is 'what' you did and 'how' you did these things that is important so check that your examples meet the positive indicators in the description of each competency.

Stage 3 – Completing the Application Form

You should now be in a position to complete the Application Form. Ensure that you prepare a rough draft of what you intend to put into the form before you begin to fill it in as there is no sense in spoiling the form. Take particular care with the competency questions as outlined in chapter 2. Only when you are happy with the form should you consider submitting it.

Stage 4 – Physical Fitness

Often candidates think that the physical fitness test is such a long way off that they leave their training too late. That approach is flawed. Examine the requirements and then go to your local gym or contact your chosen force to see if you can undergo the physical tests. Normally this is not a problem. You will then know whether you can do the exercises to the required standard. If you have any problems you will need to put together a training programme to reach the required standards and to maintain them. Most gyms and some forces will help you put together a training programme tailored to your needs. You might also want to check that your BMI falls within the acceptable limits. If not, you may have to lose some weight or build some muscle.

Stage 5 – Numerical and Verbal Logical Reasoning Tests

As with the physical fitness test it is time to assess your ability in arithmetic and comprehension. Do some of the timed tests and see how you get on. You will soon discover whether you need to brush up on your skills in these areas. If you are having some difficulties go back to basics. You can also contact your local college and get enrolled on a basic skills access course. Once you have achieved the level required continue to practice on a weekly basis to maintain your skills.

Stage 6 – Written Tests

These are the most challenging of all the tests and require plenty of preparation and practice. The emphasis must be on developing a structured approach. Your handwriting must be legible and your spelling, punctuation and grammar must be good. It should also be remembered that you will only have 20 minutes to read information, assimilate it and produce your script. This means the exercise is as much about your practical writing skills as your intellectual capacity to produce a well thought through script. You should practice weekly producing letters and reports as outlined in chapter 8 within the 20 minute limit. If you are having difficulty you can always get assistance with writing skills at your local college as indicated in the previous paragraph.

Stage 7 – Interactive Scenarios

For most people these are the most difficult and unknown area. The approach to dealing with the interactive scenarios is outlined in chapter 7.

This is a good starting point and provides a much needed framework; but, thinking the likely scenarios through on paper is not enough. At the Assessment Centre you will have to put on a good interactive performance. It follows that as you are going to 'perform' the best preparation is to do it. Candidates who have been involved in customer service work or had to deal with the public and their problems will find the interactive scenarios a little easier. The ability to interact effectively is key to this. Experience shows that working in occupations like shop assistant, bar staff, door staff, cabin crew, airline check in, security staff, benefits counter staff, waiting staff and any role that has to provide customer service and deal with complaints will be of great benefit. If you have never been involved in this type of work it might be a good idea to get some experience on a part-time basis. Remember, the Assessment Centre is designed to identify people who have the required skills and can demonstrate them.

Stage 8 – Competency Based Interview

Most candidates fear the interview. There are two reasons for this. Firstly, the difficulty of trying to find the right examples under the competency headings and, secondly, the ability to speak for 5 minutes. Generally these fears quickly disappear after you have been through the matching process in chapter 5 and you have spent some time planning and developing your answers as described in chapter 6.

It is important that you do not dismiss ideas for scenarios that you feel are not 'dynamic' enough; often the simple examples are the best. Also, you will find that preparation will produce some good material and, before you know it, you will have 15 minutes of material that you will have to squeeze into 5 minutes. Do not panic about the interview, just spend plenty of time thinking it over, put your answers together and practice with a friend by speaking out the answers to them.

If you go through these stages you will soon build an understanding of what is required, your confidence will grow and much of the stress associated with such a complex selection process will be alleviated. By creating a feeling that you are in control, your preparation will be of a high quality and your performance at the Assessment Centre will be good. Experience has shown that preparation in the months and weeks leading up to an assessment will pay dividends.

How to Prepare For the Big Day

In the final 2-3 weeks leading up to your assessment day it is important to prepare yourself mentally for the challenge. This is very important in relation to the Interactive Scenarios and the Written Exercises. You must read, understand and 'become' a newly appointed Customer Services Officer at the Westshire Centre. Read the 'Welcome Pack' carefully, know your role, the policies and other information it provides.

Good advice is to be yourself on the day but also project yourself into the role of Customer Services Officer. By doing this you will act and think professionally.

It is important that you dress and speak professionally. Women should wear a trouser suit with a high neckline with minimal jewellery and makeup. Men should wear a suit, a collar and tie and minimal jewellery. In both cases hair should be well groomed and shoes should be shiny. Visible body piercing of lips, tongues, eyebrows and noses are not appropriate. If you think this view is dated take a look at people who are employed in professional jobs, in particular police officers and the evidence speaks for itself. The issue is not one of personal prejudice but what the public generally think about the image of a police officer with facial piercings. You will be judged against these standards in the various exercises so it is good idea to try and create a good impression.

In the same way it is important to use appropriate language. Regional UK, and accents that originate outside the UK, are not a problem but you should speak clearly and adjust your expressions to meet the needs of the recipient. For example, if you are a cockney, there is no good speaking of the 'apple and pears' if the recipient will not understand that you mean 'the stairs'. Do not use slang, abusive or derogatory terms at any time. The best policy is to use clear simple expressions that everyone will understand.

Final Advice

Find yourself a mentor. Perhaps a work colleague, a partner, relative or a good friend who will help you with your development. It is always really good to have someone who will give you constructive feed back on your performance. They will be useful in helping you practice the scenarios and the interview. They can read your written work and give you ideas on solutions to problems and to check your spelling, punctuation and grammar. Never be too proud to ask someone to help and never think that you can do this all on your own. In any case, it is someone with whom you can celebrate your success when you receive the Assessment Centre results. Good luck with your preparation. I wish you every success in achieving your ambition to join the police service.

Numerical Tests

Test 1

1. What percentage of cash was stolen from the till if there was £200 at the outset and £20 after the theft?

A	B	C	D	E
90%	60%	30%	10%	15%

Answer...

2. Shopkeepers were surveyed in a town centre to discover how many premises had alarm systems. A ¼ of 280 shops did not have any alarm. How many did have an alarm?

A	B	C	D	E
270	200	260	210	180

Answer...

3. The budget for redecorating a room is £500. The undercoat paint costs £10.50, gloss paint

£15.50, sandpaper £4.00 and three rolls of wall paper £25.00. How much is left for carpeting the room?

A	B	C	D	E
£445	£380	£400	£480	£455

Answer...

4. If a coal lorry carries 56 bags of coal, how many journeys to the coal yard would be required to supply 896 bags of coal to customers?

A	B	C	D	E
18	16	19	15	12

Answer...

5. If a shed requires 4.75 litres of preservative to cover it, how much would be required to give it three coats?

A	B	C	D	E
12.50	13.25	14.25	16.45	12.25

Answer...

6. The town bus company purchased 10 large buses each having an average cost of £5000. If the company purchase 10 small buses costing £2000 each, what would be the average cost of all the buses?

A	B	C	D	E
£4000	£5000	£4000	£3000	£3500

Answer...

7. If a fish and chip meal costs £5.25, how much would 6 meals cost?

A	B	C	D	E
£31.20	£28.50	£30.50	£30.25	£31.50

Answer...

8. The local garage employs 13 mechanics. The monthly overtime bill is £850. How much will the garage have to pay over a 6 month period?

A	B	C	D	E
£4,800	£5,100	£5,050	£5,000	£4,900

Answer...

9. A council worker earns £400 per week. She is given a pay rise of 5%. What would her weekly wage be with the increase?

A	B	C	D	E
£410	£420	£450	£480	£445

Answer...

10. In a linen factory a 1/3 of the workforce of 360 is over the age of 40. How many are under 40?

A	B	C	D	E
200	190	240	230	250

Answer...

11. A lorry can be serviced at a local garage in 1½ hours if 4 mechanics work on it. How long will it take for 1 mechanic to complete the same service?

A	B	C	D	E
31/2 hrs	3 hrs	51/2 hrs	6 hrs	5 hrs

Answer...

12. If 6 police community support officers visit the local Chinese restaurant and the total bill is £150.00, how much will each pay if the bill is shared equally?

A	B	C	D	E
£22.00	£20.00	£30.00	£35.00	£25.00

Answer...

13. A police constable works 7am – 3pm for 6 days but is required to work 1½ hours overtime each day. How many hours will have been worked?

A	B	C	D	E
52 hrs	51 hrs	54 hrs	57 hrs	50 hrs

Answer...

14. A rectangular garden lawn measures 20 metres by 8 metres. If two square flower beds are created, each measuring 5 metres by 5 metres, how many square metres of lawn will remain?

A	B	C	D	E
120	110	100	80	90

Answer...

15. A beat police officer walks an average of 8 miles per shift. She works for 21 days per month. How many miles will she cover in 6 months

A   B   C   D   E
1,008   960   1,000   1,020   980

Answer...

16. If you purchase a loaf of bread costing £1.80, a pint of milk costing 98p, a tin of tomato soup costing £1.20 and a tin of beans £1.35, how much change will you get from a £10.00 note?

A   B   C   D   E
£4.30   £5.87   £5.42   £5.26   £4.67

Answer...

17. If you drive your car for 1½ hours and cover 45 miles, what is your average speed?

A   B   C   D   E
35 mph   30 mph   42 mph   20 mph   25 mph

Answer...

18. You purchase a bag of flower weighing 2 kg, a tin of beans weighing 0.5 kg, tomatoes weighing 2.4 kg, potatoes weighing 5 kg and apples weighing 2.4 kg. How many kg are in your shopping bag?

A	B	C	D	E
10.8 kg	11.4 kg	12.3 kg	12 kg	11.5 kg

Answer...

19. An oil tank capacity is 180 litres. It has 125 litres in the tank. How much will it cost to fill up the tank at 30 pence per litre?

A	B	C	D	E
£15.80	£15.50	£14.50	£14.80	£16.50

Answer...

20. A library has 60 people reading books. If 40% are men how many are women?

A	B	C	D	E
36	40	42	30	32

Answer...

21. If a paving slab measuring 1m by 1m weighs 20 kg, what would be the weight of slabs required to pave an area 10 m by 10 m?

A	B	C	D	E
2010 kg	1900 kg	1800 kg	1500 kg	2000 kg

Answer...

22. What is the average mark scored by the top 5 pupils in a school examination if they scored 80%, 75%, 70%, 65% and 45%?

A	B	C	D	E
50%	54%	67%	46%	52%

Answer...

23. A painter and decorator has 100 litres of paint. If a room requires 15 litres to cover it, how many rooms of the same size can be painted?

A	B	C	D	E
6 2/3	5 1/2	6 1/3	6	5 2/3

Answer...

24. What percentage of 55 is 33?

A	B	C	D	E
55%	60%	40%	50%	45%

Answer...

25. How many 8 cm sq tiles will be required to cover an area of 104 cm sq?

A	B	C	D	E
2.5	13	9	12	13.5

Answer...

Test 2

1. A housing estate consists of streets with the following number of houses on them 22, 32, 45, 65, 70 and 30. What is the average number of houses on each street in the estate?

A   B   C   D   E
36   38   40   44   42

Answer...

2. A motorist was caught by a speed camera travelling at 44.5 mph in a 30 mph speed restriction area. By how much was the motorist exceeding the speed limit?

A   B   C   D   E
14 mph 10 mph 14.5 mph 12.5 mph 12 mph

Answer...

3. A motoring enthusiast spends 60% of his weekly wage of £450 on motor vehicle restoration. How much does he spend per month on his hobby?

A   B   C   D   E
£1120 £1080 £960 £980 £1000

Answer...

4. A garden is 80 metres square. If a flower border 5 metres by 8 metres is established, how much garden remains?

A	B	C	D	E
44 sq m	42 sq m	45 sq m	35 sq m	40 sq m

Answer...

5. A police constable worked on a crime investigation for 18 hours out of 24 hours. What percentage of the day did she work?

A	B	C	D	E
75%	65%	55%	45%	25%

Answer...

6. A security Officer starts work at 5.30 am and works until 3.15 pm. How many hours has he worked?

A	B	C	D	E
7½	8¾	9¾	10¼	9¼

Answer...

7. A cyclist raising money for charity travels 2 miles every 12 minutes. If she cycles for 4 hours, how far will she have travelled?

A	B	C	D	E
40 miles	48 miles	50 miles	42 miles	52 miles

Answer...

8. Don's meeting will last nearly an hour and a half. Parking for 15 minutes was 40p, how much should he put in the meter?

A	B	C	D	E
£3	£2	£1.60	£1.80	£2.40

Answer...

9. A lorry maintains a speed of 52 mph travelling along the M6 motorway. How far will it travel in 1¾ hours?

A	B	C	D	E
98 miles	85 miles	91 miles	90 miles	80 miles

Answer...

10. At the local dog racing track 60% of the spectators are in the main stand. How many of the 2,000 people attending the event are not in the main stand?

A   B   C   D   E
950   850   900   800   750

Answer...

11. A loft conversion has 2 walls measuring 2 m by 4.5 m and 2 walls measuring 1.5 m by 3 m. How much plaster board will be required to cover the walls?

A   B   C   D   E
20 m   23.5 m   22.5 m   27 m   24.5 m

Answer...

12. At a local police station there are 120 officers available for patrol duties. The number available on each shift is 30. There are 3 shifts each 24 hours. What percentage is patrolling through the 24 hour period?

A   B   C   D   E
75%   60%   65%   55%   45%

Answer...

13. Four brothers are aged 4, 9, 13, and 17. What is the total of their ages?

A	B	C	D	E
43	41	39	40	42

Answer...

14. During a shopping excursion in the town centre a shopper spends £29.99, £13.40, £13.99 and £3.49 on different items. How much change will she get from £100 note?

A	B	C	D	E
£59.99	£39.13	£49.87	£50	£49

Answer...

15. A detective constable is engaged on a murder enquiry and works the following hours in the first 3 days: 5.15 am to 8.15 pm, 8.45 am to 9.45 pm, and 8 am to 8 pm. How many hours has the detective worked?

A	B	C	D	E
41	36	38	40	43

Answer...

16. A motorcyclist takes 12 hours to travel 720 miles. What is the average speed?

A   B   C   D   E
48 mph   45 mph   60 mph   50 mph   55 mph

Answer...

17. Four shops in a street were broken into overnight and property stolen to the value of £139, £377, £200 and £125. What is the total?

A   B   C   D   E
£757   £841   £650   £800   £832

Answer...

18. There are 25 football teams in the league. 20% are on their way down and 40% are on their way up. How many teams are maintaining their position?

A   B   C   D   E
15   10   5   8   6

Answer...

19. If you subtract 99,997 from 109,233, what is the figure arrived at?

A	B	C	D	E
9,236	8,230	9,770	983	8,760

Answer...

20. Los Angeles is 8 hours behind London GMT. If the time in London is 3 am and the clocks are put forward 1 hour to British Summer Time, what time is it in Los Angeles?

A	B	C	D	E
10.30 pm	9 pm	9.30 pm	7 pm	10 pm

Answer...

21. A jar of sweets was won by a class of 18 children. There were 396 sweets, how many would each child receive?

A	B	C	D	E
18	22	24	26	20

Answer...

22. How much change should a shop assistant give to a customer who pays with a £20 note for three items costing £2.87, £5.72, and £8.99?

A	B	C	D	E
£5	£2.42	£3.40	£2.40	£3.00

Answer...

23. A plot of land is 220 square metres. The house covers 80 sq m and the shed is 3 m by 2 m. How much land is available for garden?

A	B	C	D	E
134 sq m	200 sq m	86 sq m	100 sq m	90 sq m

Answer...

24. A gardener has to dig a 125 square metre plot of land with a spade. On the first day 55 square metres are dug. On the second day 45 square metres are dug. What percentage remains to be dug?

A	B	C	D	E
25%	30%	33%	40%	20%

Answer...

25. A Swallow can fly at 30 mph when there is no wind blowing. If the bird has to fly into an oncoming wind of 10 mph, how far will it travel in 3½ hours?

A	B	C	D	E
55 miles	60 miles	70 miles	75 miles	65 miles

Answer...

Test 3

1. A taxi company charges £2.50 for 4 minutes travel. If a journey takes 32 minutes, how much will the fare be?

A	B	C	D	E
£22	£12	£20	£18	£12.50

Answer...

2. It takes 5¾ hours to drive a car between 2 large cities. If you stop after 1¼ hours for refreshments and then again after 3½ hours, how much time is left before you arrive at your destination?

A	B	C	D	E
1 hr	1¾ hr	1¼ hr	2 hr	2¼ hr

Answer...

3. Sheep sell at market for £35.50 each. A farmer has a flock of 100 sheep to sell but 20% are sick and cannot be sold. How much money will the farmer get from those that he can sell?

A	B	C	D	E
£2,840	£1,670	£2,640	£2,300	£1,300

Answer...

4. 30 free range chickens are laying 1 egg on 3 days per week and 18 chickens are laying 1 egg on 4 days per week. How many eggs are laid each week?

A	B	C	D	E
152	162	143	150	168

Answer...

5. A cross-country runner can run 1 mile in 6 minutes. If she starts running at 10.30 am and finishes at 12 noon, how many miles has the runner covered?

A	B	C	D	E
17	14	15	18	16

Answer...

6. A postal worker delivers letters each day and walks, on average, 40 metres per letter. If there are 250 letters to deliver, how far will they walk?

A	B	C	D	E
10,000 m	9,800 m	10,120 m	9,700 m	10,100 m

Answer...

7. New York is 5 hours behind London GMT. The clocks in London are put forward 1 hour at 3 am on a Sunday morning. What time is it in New York?

A	B	C	D	E
10 pm	11 pm	7 pm	10.3 pm	9 pm

Answer...

8. If 1 man can row a boat 1½ miles in 2 hours, how long will it take 3 men to row the same distance?

A	B	C	D	E
3 hr	30 mins	40 mins	15 mins	1 hr

Answer:...

9. An aircraft travelling at 625 mph into a head wind of 120 mph. How far will the aircraft travel in 1 hour?

A	B	C	D	E
305 m	405 m	505 m	745 m	625 m

Answer...

10. What percentage of 625 is 125?

A	B	C	D	E
40%	35%	25%	20%	30%

Answer...

11. Bill buys a radio for £18.99, headphones £3.94 and an extension lead for £5.99. How much has he spent?

A	B	C	D	E
£28.92	£29.82	£28.97	£26.92	£25.98

Answer...

12. Three out of 12 cars are stopped by police at a check point. Out of 156 cars how many were stopped?

A	B	C	D	E
39	45	35	48	41

Answer...

13. How much would it cost to purchase 3 loaves of bread at 59 pence each?

A	B	C	D	E
£1.62	£1.72	£1.74	£1.77	£1.57

Answer...

14. A nurse starts work at 5.45 am and works for 10 hours. What time will he finish work?

A	B	C	D	E
1.45 pm	2.45 pm	3.45 pm	4.45 pm	1.30 pm

Answer...

15. If you purchase a sandwich for £2.05, a coffee for 95p and a chocolate bar for 33p, how much will you have spent?

A	B	C	D	E
£2.45	£3.45	£3.33	£3.30	£3.00

Answer...

16. If you travel on the train for 58 minutes and by taxi for 37 minutes, how long is the journey?

A	B	C	D	E
1 hr 30 m	1 hr 35 m	1 hr 31 m	1 hr 25 m	1 hr

Answer...

17. If 7 cars fill up from a petrol pump and a total of 315 litres are extracted, how much has each car taken on average?

A	B	C	D	E
45 litres	35 litres	39 litres	43 litres	47 litres

Answer...

18. A harbour has 860 berths for boats. A 1/5 of them are motor boats. How many other boats are there?

A	B	C	D	E
1,1032	688	960	788	786

Answer...

19. A factory worker earns £450 per week, how much will he earn in 7 weeks?

A	B	C	D	E
£2,750	£2,700	£3,450	£3, 350	£3,150

Answer...

20. A long distance runner completed 20 miles in 120 minutes, what is his average speed per mile?

A	B	C	D	E
6 mph	7 mph	7.5 mph	6.5 mph	10 mph

Answer...

21. Jim spends £5.50 on lunch and £4.75 for afternoon tea at a motorway service station. How much has he spent?

A	B	C	D	E
£9.95	£9.15	£10.45	£10.25	£9.95

Answer...

22. Ben's car cost £2,500, car tax was £155 and insurance was £780. What is the cost of his motoring so far?

A	B	C	D	E
£3345	£3425	£3435	£3245	£3525

Answer...

23. The total restaurant bill was £37.92, if the wine cost £6.99 how much was the food?

A	B	C	D	E
£44.91	£30.93	£31.93	£30.91	£30.99

Answer...

24. The gateau was cut into 24 slices; Sam ate 25% of the gateau, how many slices were left?

A	B	C	D	E
6	8	12	16	18

Answer...

25. 30 conifer trees are planted 2 metres apart along a garden fence to create a hedge. How long is the garden fence?

A	B	C	D	E
60 m	58 m	56 m	62 m	64 m

Answer...

Test 4

1. 30 children need new text books which cost £3.74 each. What is the total cost?

A   B   C   D   E
£112.20   £111.20   £112.50   £142.20   £104.10

Answer...

2. The local supermarket runs a special deal on French wine and reduces the price on each bottle by 40%. What would be the price of a bottle costing £6.00?

A   B   C   D   E
£2.60   £3.60   £3.00   £3.20   £3.10

Answer...

3. An aircraft leaves London at 7.30 pm and travels to Washington DC in the USA, which is 5 hours behind London time. What would be the local time in Washington when the aircraft lands if the journey takes 6 hours?

A   B   C   D   E
3 pm   2.30 pm   8.30 pm   4.30 pm   5.30 pm

Answer...

4. Gym membership costs £540 for one year. This will rise by 15% for next year. What will the new membership costs be?

A	B	C	D	E
£594	£694	£621	£651	£626

Answer...

5. The discount card gave 20% off everything. Maggie bought goods to the value of £450, how much was the final bill?

A	B	C	D	E
£90	£360	£390	£350	£320

Answer...

6. If you multiply 200 by 100 and divide by 50, what is the sum?

A	B	C	D	E
204	303	400	355	300

Answer...

7. If the pressure on the surface of the sea is 1 bar and for every 10 metres that a diver descends into the sea the pressure increases by 1 bar. What will be the pressure at 40 metres?

A	B	C	D	E
3 bar	7 bar	6 bar	5 bar	4 bar

Answer...

8. If the fence along the side of a field has 25 posts and the gap between the posts is 2 metres, how long is the fence?

A	B	C	D	E
48 m	50 m	35 m	45 m	38 m

Answer...

9. A tap fills a bath at 25 litres per minute. How long will it take to fill a bath with 600 litres of water?

A	B	C	D	E
24 min	22 min	26 min	28 min	21 min

Answer...

10. A river flows downstream at 3 knots. A canoe can be paddled at a speed of 5 knots in slack water. How fast will the canoe travel down stream?

A	B	C	D	E
2 knots	5 knots	8 knots	3 knots	4 knots

Answer...

11. During a heavy rain storm a house roof 5 metres by 3 metres sheds 30 litres of water. If the roof of the house next door has shed 10 litres of water, what is the area of the roof?

A	B	C	D	E
5 sq m	8 sq m	10 sq m	6 sq m	4 sq m

Answer...

12. A ball rolling down a hill increases speed by a 1/3 every 10 metres. If the speed of the ball is 21 mph after 20 metres, how fast will it be travelling after 30 metres?

A	B	C	D	E
35 mph	25 mph	42 mph	28 mph	44 mph

Answer...

13. The price of a pot of jam is increased by 20% to £1.20. What was the original price of the jam?

A	B	C	D	E
70p	60p	90p	80p	£1.00

Answer...

14. A lawn is 130 metres by 70 metres. The lawn mower has a cut width of 1 metre and it takes 1½ minutes to cut a 130 metre strip of grass. How long will it take to cut the whole lawn?

A	B	C	D	E
1 hr 45 m	1 hr 35 m	1 hr 20 m	1 hr	1 hr 5 m

Answer...

15. A cinema can seat 500 people. During a mid-week performance 350 people are in attendance. As a percentage how many seats were unfilled?

A	B	C	D	E
20%	15%	25%	35%	30%

Answer...

16. A length of rope is 20 metres long. How many 25 centimetre lengths can be cut from the rope?

A	B	C	D	E
60	50	75	80	85

Answer...

17. How much will it cost to buy 1,000 envelopes at 27 pence each?

A	B	C	D	E
270	250	245	230	235

Answer...

18. A bank account has the following amounts withdrawn on three consecutive days: £135, £77 and £173. What is the total withdrawn?

A	B	C	D	E
£275	£265	£245	£285	£385

Answer...

19. At a busy roundabout there are, on average, 4 accidents every 3 days. How many accidents, on average, will there be over a 21 day period?

A	B	C	D	E
24	25	26	28	18

Answer...

20. A professional footballer trains in the gym for 1¼ hours each day. How long does the footballer spend in the gym over a 7 day period?

A	B	C	D	E
6½ hrs	8¾ hrs	7¼ hrs	7¾ hrs	7½ hrs

Answer...

21. A steel chain costs £3.25 per metre. How much will 7 metres cost?

A	B	C	D	E
£22.75	£18.00	£18.75	£21.75	£23.75

Answer...

22. A photocopier can print 40 copies per minute. How long will it take to print 500 copies?

A	B	C	D	E
11.5 min	12.5 min	14.5 min	13.5 min	10 min

Answer...

23. The cost of a mans haircut is £8.50 and a boys haircut is £6.50. If 15 men and 3 boys have haircuts, how much is taken?

A	B	C	D	E
£127.50	£137	£147	£127	£117

Answer...

24. How long will it take to drive 125 miles at a speed of 50 mph?

A	B	C	D	E
3 hrs	1½ hrs	1¾ hrs	2½ hrs	2¾ hrs

Answer...

25. A box containing 8 tins of dog meat costs £10.00. How much will 3 tins cost?

A	B	C	D	E
£2.75	£3.75	£1.75	£4.75	£5.75

Answer...

Numerical Tests - Answers

	Test 1	Test 2	Test 3	Test 4
1	A	D	C	A
2	D	C	A	B
3	A	B	A	C
4	B	E	B	C
5	C	A	C	B
6	E	C	A	C
7	E	A	A	D
8	B	E	C	A
9	B	C	C	A
10	C	D	D	C
11	D	D	A	A
12	E	A	A	D
13	D	A	D	E
14	B	B	C	A
15	A	D	C	E
16	E	C	B	D
17	B	B	A	A
18	C	B	B	E
19	E	A	E	D
20	A	D	E	B
21	E	B	D	A
22	C	B	C	B
23	A	A	B	C
24	B	E	E	D
25	B	C	B	B

Appendix 2

Verbal logical Reasoning Tests

Test 1

At 2 am on Saturday morning a Rover motor car veered off a main road and collided with a wall. The car burst into flames. There was one victim who was killed in the crash. She has been identified as Marjorie Hibbert who lived in the village of Angel two miles away. It is also known that:

- A dead cat was found near the crash scene
- The drive from Marjorie's house to the Lantern Restaurant took 10 minutes
- The waiter at the restaurant served Marjorie and her friend during the evening
- Marjorie visits the restaurant every Tuesday

1. Marjorie was over the legal alcohol limit at 2 am ( )
2. Marjorie swerved to avoid hitting the cat ( )
3. Marjorie was on her way home when she was killed ( )
4. Marjorie was alone in the car when she was killed ( )
5. Marjorie was a regular visitor at the Lantern Restaurant ( )

A = True   B = False   C = Impossible to say

The Post Office in Bramwell had three masked men, with guns, demand money from the cashiers at 10 am on Monday 1st August. They escaped in an old grey Volvo car but were apprehended by the police a few streets away and the money was recovered. It is also known that:

- One shot was heard
- The police arrested and charged three men
- Police were at the scene two minutes after the alarm was raised
- Customers were told to lie on the floor whilst the cashiers put the money in bags
- No injuries were sustained
- There were two cashiers and six customers

6. A customer was shot ( )
7. A passer-by raised the alarm ( )
8. There were three thieves ( )
9. Customers had to lie on the floor during the robbery ( )
10. There was a chase through the streets of Bramwell ( )

On 10th October two brothers were found dead in the garden shed at their home. The cause of death was unknown. It is also known that:

- A youth was see near the back garden on 9th October
- The victims were Charles and Stuart Glover aged 14 and 12
- The two deaths were discovered by the brother's father, David Glover
- David Glover stored solvents in his shed connected with his paint spraying business
- The two boys were known to have purchased solvent based glue from a local hardware shop
- Two boys were caught sniffing glue by teachers at the local comprehensive school

11. The two boys died from suffocation ( )
12. The boy's father had specifically told them not to touch the solvents in the shed ( )
13. Charles and Stuart were caught sniffing glue a school ( )
14. The boys may have died from sniffing solvents ( )
15. The police were called by David Glover ( )

James Matheson was arrested following a police raid on his home. A number of cannabis plants were found in the roof space and a number of tablets were found under a cushion in a lounge chair. Some electrical tools were recovered from the garage. It is also known that:

- James Matheson was cautioned for possessing cannabis 2 years ago
- A lodger, Fred French, has lived with James Matheson for two years
- Fred French has previous convictions for handling stolen goods
- James Matheson was seen unloading things from his car into the garage two days ago
- James Matheson denies knowledge of the cannabis plants and electrical tools
- A number of callers have been see speaking to James Matheson and taking away small packets

16. Fred French stole the electrical goods ( )
17. James Matheson may have cultivated the cannabis plants ( )
18. James has been charged with possession of cannabis ( )
19. Fred French has previously been arrested for handling stolen goods ( )
20. Another lodger is responsible for the drugs and stolen electrical goods ( )

A mother and son were found dead in their flat in Redditch. They had been poisoned and police are investigating the circumstances. It is also known that:

- The victims were Angela Cross, aged 26 and Neil Cross, aged 3
- Nigel Cross, the estranged husband of Angela, had been released from prison
- Angela's new partner, Michael Moor, aged 42, reported the deaths at 6.30 pm on Tuesday 27th August
- Angela and Neil had both tested positive for HIV

21. Angela could have poisoned Neil   ( )
22. Nigel Cross is a carrier of AIDS   ( )
23. Neil was a healthy boy when he died   ( )
24. Michael was the first person to find
      the two bodies   ( )
25. Angela was frightened of her husband   ( )

Ben Ford, aged 11, was to collect his younger brother, William, aged 6, from the Infant School playground after school on Wednesday. School finishes at 3.25 pm. William could not be found on the school premises and Ben was concerned. Their mother had a dental appointment and was unable to meet the boys from school. It is also known that:

- William was seen looking at a book at 3.30 pm by the school caretaker.
- On Tuesday William's class had choir practice after school with a new music teacher
- The music teacher said that William was collected by his mother at 4 pm
- A tall, blonde woman was seen reading with William in the playground.
- William's mother has bright auburn hair and is 5 feet tall.
- School policy is for Infant School children to be collected by a parent.

26. William was taken home by his mother ( )
27. Ben was late to meet his brother. ( )
28. Ben and William are great friends. ( )
29. The caretaker is responsible for making sure that all children are collected ( )
30. The school is inadequate in carrying out its duties ( )
31. Ben may have gone to the school on the wrong day ( )

Test 2

On Saturday 14th June the maintenance woman for the Bourne Bowls Club discovered that the green had been damaged. In consequence, the afternoon bowls match had to be cancelled. On Monday the police discovered the damage had been caused by motorcyclists performing 'wheelies'. It is also known:

- The maintenance woman is a motorcycle enthusiast
- Samuel James owns a motor cycle
- A group of youths had an altercation with a Bowls Club member on Friday evening
- A club member had recently been expelled from the club for abusive behaviour
- The maintenance woman was the only person with access to the green when the club was closed

1. The group of youths may have entered the club and caused the damage   ( )
2. The maintenance woman new the people responsible for the damage   ( )
3. The expelled club member caused the damage with a friend   ( )
4. The maintenance woman asked the youths to inflict the damage and gave them access   ( )
5. Samuel may have been one of the youths causing the damage   ( )

A = True   B = False   C = Impossible to say

A man, aged 38, was involved in a hit and run incident in Padstow on 15th July at 12.15 pm and was badly injured. The police were unable to trace the black van described by the witness. It is also known that:

- The injured man was identified as Tom Burton, a local solicitor
- Tom is involved with planning applications for building contracts for the council
- Two mothers in Padstow reported a speeding black van outside the local school at lunchtime
- Tom was on annual leave for the week

6. Tom Burton is a solicitor ( )
7. Tom was injured during his lunch break from work ( )
8. A black builders van was stolen ( )
9. Tom was knocked down outside the School ( )
10. Tom's girlfriend has children ( )

At 2.30 pm on 2nd February a robbery occurred at Pains Jewellers in the High Street. The offender had a sawn off shotgun and shouted the word 'now' as he told the owner what to do. He escaped in a red car that was parked outside on double yellow lines. The police recovered a red car abandoned one mile away. It is also known:

- Jimmy James crashed his car at 2.45 pm
- The shop assistant was a woman and 5'11" tall
- The robber was taller the shop assistant
- Greg Johnston drove the getaway car from the robbery
- Fred Giles was 5'5" tall
- A Traffic Warden was issuing a ticket to the red car as the robber ran out of the shop carrying the shotgun

11. The Traffic Warden may have called the police	( )
12. Fred Giles was the robber	( )
13. Jimmy James was the getaway car driver	( )
14. The shop assistant knew the robber	( )
15. Gold and silver jewellery was stolen during the robbery	( )

A bungalow was completely destroyed by a fire in the early hours of Wednesday morning. A neighbour opposite heard an explosion and on looking out of the window saw a tall man in his 50's run away from the seat of the explosion. It is also known that:

- The owner of the bungalow was James Sheehan, aged 54
- There was no forced entry to the property
- A planning application had just been granted to knock down the bungalow and build a five bedroom house
- The bungalow was insured for knock down and rebuild in the event of structural damage
- Harry Shand was in Ireland on Wednesday night
- James Sheehan could not afford to have the bungalow dismantled by a demolition company
- A gas leak had been reported the previous day

16. James Sheehan may have conspired to defraud his insurance company by having the bungalow burnt down ( )
17. Harry Shand burnt the bungalow down using petrol to start the fire ( )
18. A gas explosion caused the fire ( )
19. A tramp broke the lock off the back door and entered the property to stay overnight. ( )
20. Demolition was not necessary ( )

A woman, aged 35, was found dead alongside a car in an isolated beauty spot car park. A subsequent post mortem examination established she died of carbon monoxide poisoning. It is also known that:

- The woman was identified as Angela Spark by her mother
- Angela's husband recently died of cancer following a long illness
- Angela had run up considerable debts during the period of her husbands illness
- She was expected to receive substantial insurance payments following her husbands death
- Richard, Angela's only child, was aware of the substantial insurance payments and would inherit them one day
- Richard and his mother had not seen each other for many years following an argument

21. Angela may have committed suicide ( )
22. Angela's father died several years ago ( )
23. Richard had called to see his mother
    the night before she died ( )
24. Angela was identified by her brother ( )
25. Richard had a sister ( )

Three laptops were taken from cars parked outside the cinema, during the evening of 20th May. Eight cars were broken into during the evening. It is also known that:

- All of the cars had the front passenger side window broken
- A local publican reported that a laptop, car stereo and mobile phone were being offered for sale by Jim Martin
- Three youths were seen running from the car park when alarms were heard
- Jim Martin has a previous conviction for car theft

26. Jim Martin may have stolen the laptops ( )
27. The thefts were probably carried out by
     the same person(s)   ( )
28. Three men were involved in the thefts ( )
29. The items for sale in the pub were stolen ( )
30. Each car was broken into because of a
     laptop on display   ( )
31. Bill Bones was one of the thieves   ( )

Test 3

Mrs Kent, aged 79, left home at 9 am and returned at 11.30 am. She discovered a window had been broken at the rear and an untidy search of the house had been carried out. Jewellery was stolen from a dressing table. The police investigation has uncovered the following facts:

- Mrs Kent's grandson, Sam, visited her frequently
- A neighbour saw a tall man dressed in black visit the house at 10.30 am and minutes later saw him run off down the road
- Mrs Kent's house was always untidy
- Sam has been convicted of burglary
- The post woman saw Sam and a friend at the front of the house at 9.45 am
- The water meter reader informed the police there were two suspicious youths at the house

1. Sam may have broken into the house and stolen the jewellery ( )
2. The neighbour called the police ( )
3. The house may not have been broken into by a burglar ( )
4. The tall man in black is the main suspect ( )
5. The neighbour's children broke the window with their ball ( )

A = True   B = False   C = Impossible to say

On Thursday morning at 8.45 am the train from the city crossed an unmanned level crossing and struck a blue car. The driver was killed. The police uncovered the following facts:

- Two youths were seen placing large rocks on the track the night before
- A witness said when the train hit the blue car it was stationary on the crossing
- It was known that the driver of the blue car was late for work
- A passenger on the train said it was derailed and veered off the track colliding with the blue car
- The car driver had substantial credit card debts

6. The blue car may have been driven onto the track deliberately ( )
7. The two youths were responsible for derailing the train and causing the accident ( )
8. The engine of the blue car stalled as it crossed the track ( )
9. The car driver may have taken a risk and tried to cross before the train got to the crossing ( )
10. The gates on the unmanned crossing were broken ( )

A carer reported that Marjorie Davies, aged 93, was found dead at home, in the kitchen, early one morning. Police are investigating. It is also known that:

- Marjorie was frail, reclusive, rather deaf and devoted to her cats
- A cat's home is a beneficiary of her will
- The carer had attended every morning for the last three years
- Marjorie has a niece and nephew that she hasn't seen for several years
- A neighbour reported that a couple had been seen knocking at Marjorie's door the previous evening
- Letters and cards sent from Australia for 'Auntie Marj' were found

11. Marjorie Davies may have died of
      natural causes   ( )
12. Marjorie had a close relationship with
      her family   ( )
13. Marjorie knew the couple knocking at
      the door   ( )
14. Marjorie had died after tripping over one
      of the cats   ( )
15. Marjorie often had visitors   ( )

At 3.45 pm on Friday three children were hit by a white car whilst walking home from school. The car mounted the pavement and struck a glancing blow to the three girls. They received minor injuries. The car did not stop and drove off in the direction of the town centre. The police found a white car with damage to its offside abandoned in a town centre car park. The following facts are also known:

- A white car was reported stolen at 3 pm the same day
- The children were all aged 9
- The police had received a report of a white car being driven recklessly in the area where the children were struck
- The white car had recently failed the annual MOT test

16. A white car injured the three children ( )
17. The car that struck the girls was the
      stolen car ( )
18. The children were walking home from
      school ( )
19. The owner of the car reported it stolen
      because it failed the MOT ( )
20. The car driver stopped immediately after
      the collision ( )

During the evening of 25th October the rear entrance door to the local secondary school was damaged by fire after a motor vehicle was set alight close to the building. The police are investigating what happened and discovered the following:

- The car belonged to Danny Hargreaves
- A group of children had been seen near the car smoking, chatting and messing about
- A teacher calling to pick up school books discovered the fire
- The school caretaker had recently been sacked for incompetence although he was still living in accommodation nearby
- The caretaker called the police and fire brigade

21. The caretaker set fire to the car because he was angry about being sacked ( )
22. A classroom was damaged by the fire ( )
23. The children called the fire brigade ( )
24. The car had been stolen and set on fire by the owner ( )
25. The car may have been set alight by children messing about with cigarettes ( )

During Monday night three buses were burnt out at the corporation bus depot. Two men aged in their late 40's were seen at the depot at 9.15 pm on Monday evening. One man was over 6' tall and the other was about 5'5". A police investigation uncovered the following facts:

- A short man was seen near the buses with a petrol can just before the fire
- The buses were in the depot for driver's seat upgrades
- Alan Gallagher, a bus driver, is 6'6" tall and was sacked from his job following an argument with the depot manager
- John Lewis, a good friend of Gallagher, is 5'4" and has a conviction for arson
- A witness saw three youths smoking and larking about by the depot fence adjacent to the buses
- The bus company had received threats from the Animal Liberation Front (ALF)

26. John Lewis was responsible for the fire ( )
27. Alan Gallagher decide to get his own back because he was sacked ( )
28. The buses were at the depot for bodywork repairs ( )
29. John Lewis is a burglar ( )
30. The ALF may have planted a petrol bomb on the buses ( )
31. The fire could have been started accidentally by the youths throwing cigarette stubs over the fence ( )

Test 4

At 10.30 pm the landlord of the Three Pigeons ejected a drunken man called James Franks from the pub following an altercation. At 10.45 pm a brick was thrown through the window of the pub. During the police investigation into the damage the following became clear:

- Threats had been made against the landlord after barring two men the previous week
- A witness saw two men running away from the pub just after the window smashed and called the police
- James Franks was seen staggering down the road in the opposite direction to the other two men
- Three shop windows a short distance away had been broken by a group of youths

1. A customer was injured when the brick was thrown through the window ( )
2. James Franks may have been too drunk to throw a brick through the pub window ( )
3. The group of youths was responsible for the damage ( )
4. The two men seen running away may have been barred the previous week ( )
5. The landlord called the police ( )

A = True   B = False   C = Impossible to say

At 3.30 pm an articulated lorry veered of the London Road and crashed into the front of a bungalow 50 feet from the road. Substantial damage was caused to the bungalow. It is also know that:

- The driver had been convicted of drinking and driving 4 years ago
- The speed limit on the road was 40 mph
- A black dog was seen on the road 5 minutes before the accident happened
- The lorry left Dover at 6 am and had been driven non-stop for the last six hours
- The lorry was travelling at 40 mph when the crash occurred
- There were no witnesses to the accident

6. The resident of the house was injured in the
     Crash   ( )
7. The house will have to be demolished   ( )
8. The driver was over the drink driving limit ( )
9. A witness saw a black dog run in front of the
     lorry causing it to swerve   ( )
10. The driver may have been speeding at the
     time of the accident   ( )

After the football match disorder broke out at the Swan pub between rival supporters. The police arrested 20 youths for public order offences and damage to the pub. As a result of the incident the following is known:

- The police charged 15 people with public order offences and 4 with criminal damage
- Two fans were arguing by the main door just before the disorder broke out
- Eight supporters were injured in the disorder
- The front door to the pub was damaged
- The damage amounted to £5,000
- Four police officers suffered minor injuries from making arrests

11. The injured supporters were assaulted by the opposing supporters ( )
12. The damage to the pub consisted of broken windows ( )
13. The police officers received injuries when they were attacked by supporters ( )
14. All of the people arrested were football supporters ( )
15. The trouble may have been started after an altercation between two supporters ( )

A derelict house was destroyed by fire during the early hours of Saturday morning. The body of a man was found in the remains of an upstairs bedroom in the fire damaged house. The man died of inhalation of smoke. The police are treating the fire and death as suspicious. The following facts are known:

- The dead man had high alcohol levels and would have been drunk before he died
- The fire was started at the foot of the stairs using an old mattress
- A violent argument between three men was heard by a neighbour at about 1am
- Two men were seen walking away from the house shortly before the blaze began
- The police detained a vagrant 400 metres from the house as they attended the reported fire
- The detained man had a recent burn to his right hand and had singed hair and eyebrows

16. The police do not have any suspects for the fire ( )
17. The dead man died of an assault following an argument with two men ( )
18. The police have arrested and charged the two men seen walking away with arson ( )
19. The vagrant detained by the police with burns may have started the fire ( )
20. The owner of the house started the fire so that he could make an insurance claim ( )

Alfie Griffiths, aged 91, was found dead in his flat on Sunday morning by his only visitor his neighbour Elsie Jones, aged 85. The police are investigating the circumstances of Alfie's death. It is also known that:

- Alfie complained to Elsie on Friday that he had chest pains
- He had suffered a minor heart attack three weeks before
- The flat was very untidy
- Elsie visited Alfie every two days
- A white van was seen outside the flat the previous day and a man was knocking on the door

21. Alfie was last seen on Saturday ( )
22. The flat was broken into ( )
23. Alfie may have died of a heart attack ( )
24. The milkman tried to collect milk money on Saturday ( )
25. The flat was in disarray ( )

Mary Jones went shopping in the town centre on Thursday 12th and when she returned she discovered her husband, James, dead and hanging from a rope suspended from a rafter in the garage. The police are treating the death as suspicious and have discovered the following:

- James and Mary went shopping together every Thursday morning
- They would catch the bus at 10 am and return at 1 pm.
- On Thursday 12th James decided to stay at home and catch a later bus and meet Mary for lunch at 12.30 pm but he never appeared
- James had substantial life insurance policies
- At 10.30 am a neighbour saw James and borrowed a garden fork
- James had been diagnosed with cancer and was extremely concerned how he would cope with the illness

26. The milkman called to collect payment
     at 11.15 am   ( )
27. James never went shopping with Mary   ( )
28. Mary stood to collect substantial
     sums of insurance money   ( )
29. James may have committed suicide   ( )
30. James was not seen alive after
     10.15 am   ( )
31. A neighbour saw James and Mary
     returning from shopping at 1pm   ( )

Verbal Logical Reasoning Tests - Answers

	Test 1	Test 2	Test 3	Test 4
1	C	A	A	C
2	C	C	B	A
3	C	C	A	C
4	A	C	B	C
5	A	C	C	B
6	B	A	A	C
7	C	B	C	C
8	A	C	C	C
9	A	C	A	B
10	C	C	C	B
11	C	A	A	C
12	C	B	B	B
13	C	B	C	B
14	A	C	C	C
15	C	C	B	A
16	C	A	A	B
17	A	B	C	B
18	B	C	A	C
19	A	B	C	A
20	C	B	B	C
21	A	A	C	C
22	C	C	C	C
23	B	B	B	A
24	C	B	C	C
25	C	B	A	A
26	A	A	C	C
27	C	A	C	B

28	C	C	B	A
29	C	C	B	A
30	B	B	A	B
31	A	C	A	B

Written Exercises

Shooting Star

'Shooting Star', a major electrical supplier, is having a massive promotion on electrical goods in their store. They are advertising flat screen televisions, hifi systems, digital radios and many other lines which are all blaring out excessive noise to draw attention to their products. They have all the store front doors open to attract customer's attention.

The 'Helping the Old' charity shop next door to Shooting Star is finding the noise excessive and they are unable to carry on their normal business because of the disruption being caused.

The Helping the Old store manager has complained to the manager of Shooting Star about the noise but she has refused to turn the sound down. In fact, the two managers are now in dispute and not talking to each other.

Shooting Star claims that it has every right to advertise its goods in this way because they are a large commercial business trying to make money whilst Helping the Old is just a charity shop.

You have been asked to suggest ways to resolve the issue.

Prepare a proposal report to deal with the situation.

Car Bits

'Car Bits', a major chain store, receives two deliveries of stock each week. A large lorry parks at the rear of the premises to unload.

The adjacent shop 'Carnival Biscuits' is a bakery which produces fancy biscuits and cakes. These are distributed daily from the shop to other retail outlets. Every morning a delivery van collects items from the bakery for distribution at 8.30 am.

On Tuesday and Thursday each week the Car Bits delivery is scheduled for 7.30 am. A problem has arisen on several occasions recently when the Car Bits lorry has taken until 9.30 am to unload. This has prevented access to the bakery and the collection of cakes and biscuits cannot take place.

The store managers have spoken to each other about the problem but nothing has been resolved. The bakery manager has complained to the centre manager and wants the situation resolved.

You have been asked to suggest ways of dealing with the dispute.

Prepare a proposal report to deal with the situation.

Top Notch Dogs

A top quality hot dog company, 'Top Notch Dogs', has been granted permission to stand one of its caravans in the mall adjacent to the food hall.

Since Top Notch Dogs arrived three weeks ago it has been welcomed by the traders in the shopping centre and customers have praised the quality and friendliness of the staff on the hot dog caravan. The presence of the Top Notch Dogs company has enhanced the facilities available to customers attending the shopping centre.

Despite the warm reception the hot dog company has received, a number of complaints have been received. Two stores have complained about the increasing amount of rubbish being dropped on the mall floor. Food and paper wrappings are being discarded which has led to food and tomato sauce being scattered about. This is causing a health hazard. Also, two customers have complained about slipping on tomato sauce and narrowly avoiding serious injury.

There have also been complaints about youths gathering on a seat adjacent to the hot dog caravan. They have been smoking, drinking cans of beer, shouting and using profane language.

The centre manager has asked you to propose a solution to the problems that have arisen.

Prepare a proposal report to deal with the situation.

The Tanning Salon

The recent opening of a beauty salon in the shopping centre was followed by a high profile on-going advertising campaign. This has consisted of four young women dressed in skimpy swimming costumes moving amongst shoppers in the centre distributing leaflets about the beauty treatments offered by the salon.

A number of complaints have been received by shoppers visiting the centre. A lady shopper has complained that the way in which the young women are dressed is demeaning to women. A male shopper has complained that he was approached by two of the women who put their arms around him and kissed him on both cheeks whilst a photograph was taken. He found this highly embarrassing.

Another lady of Asian origin complained to the manager of the Tanning Salon that the whole advertising campaign offended her cultural and religious beliefs. The manager allegedly told her 'this is Britain, if you don't like it you know what to do'.

The centre manager has asked you to propose a solution to this problem as she intends to speak to the Tanning Salon manager next week.

Prepare a proposal report for the centre manager to enable her to resolve the situation.

Entry Criteria for Police Constables

Age Requirements

You can apply to join the police service at the age of 18 but you cannot be appointed as a police officer until you are 18½. The upper age limit for applying to the police is not fixed. However, in view of the fact the retirement age for police constables and sergeants is 55; it is unlikely that a police force will consider an application over the age of 51.

Height Requirements

There is no height requirement.

Educational Requirements

You do not require formal qualifications to join the police service but you will have to attend an Assessment Centre to test whether you have the skills required which will include basic arithmetic and written skills.

Nationality Requirements

You must be a British Citizen, an EC/EEA national or a Commonwealth Citizen or foreign national with unrestricted access to the United Kingdom.

Tattoos

Tattoos are not acceptable if they are particularly prominent, garish and offensive or undermine the dignity and authority of the role of police constable.

Criminal Record

If you have a number of crimes recorded against you or you have been cautioned in the last five years for crimes of violence or public order offences, you are unlikely to be accepted by a police force. It will be important to contact your chosen force to ask them if they will accept an application from you if you fall into this category.

Financial Status

Registered bankrupts and those who have County Court judgments against them for outstanding debts will be rejected. If you have discharged bankruptcy debts then you will need to provide a Certificate of Satisfaction with your application.

The reason these conditions are imposed on applicants is due to the fact that police officers have access to privileged information which may make them vulnerable to corruption.

Physical Fitness

Police officers have to be fit to undertake the role and therefore applicants will have to pass a fitness test. There is a dynamic strength and endurance test that all candidates must pass before appointment.

Health

The nature of police work is inherently stressful, traumatic, physical and involves shift working. This means that officers need to be resilient enough to cope with the demands and pressures of police work. Applicants must therefore be in good health mentally and physically to undertake police duties. A medical examination will be required to determine suitability.

Eyesight

Eyesight will have to meet the required standards that will be tested at the medical examination stage. The current standards require applicants to have distance vision of 6/12, or better, with either your right or left eye and 6/6 with both eyes together. If you wear contact lenses or spectacles you need to reach 6/36 unaided. Failure to pass this test will lead to rejection. (6/36 is the second line from the top of the opticians chart, 6/12 is the fifth line and 6/6 is the seventh line)

Previous Applications

You can only apply to one force at a time. Where you have previously applied to join the police service and been unsuccessful, you must wait six months from your initial rejection before you can apply again.

Appendix 5

Frequently Asked Questions

The following is a list of frequently asked questions. This list is not exhaustive, however, it will provide you with a guide to the criteria that will be applied to applicants to the police service.

Entry Conditions

"I'm 18½ and was told by a police officer to go away and get some life experience and come back in 5 years. Am I too young to join?"

No. You can join the police at 18½ years of age. Your suitability for police work does not depend entirely on your age. Many factors play a part in developing your personality and skills. It will depend on what experiences you have had in life and what you have gained from them. The Assessment Centre is designed to test whether you have the skills and if you are able to demonstrate the required level in each of the competencies. Do not assume because you are young that you cannot become a police officer.

"At 45 I must be too old to join the police and how would I relate to all those younger officers?"

The average age of recruits joining the police service is around 27 years of age and most police forces will recruit people up to the age of 50. There is a place for people of all ages in policing. The experience of life is a vital ingredient in delivering an effective service to the community and you will not stand out because you are older. The police organisation is very mature and deals with a diverse community.

"When I left school I went to sea and had tattoos of naked women put on the back of each hand. Will I get into the police with these?"

It is unlikely that the police will accept an application from someone who has tattoos that are in any way sexist, racist, sectarian, homophobic, lewd, crude, display unacceptable attitudes to women or minority groups or alignment with a particular group. The nature of a police officers role does not allow displays that can be misinterpreted or are offensive in any way. Police forces will ask if you have tattoos and will vet them to see if they are acceptable.

"I own and live in a pub. My wife is the licencee and I don't have anything to do with the running of the business, will I be ok to apply?"

There are restrictions on the private lives of police officers and these include having a business interest. It is within the prerogative of the Chief Constable to determine whether a business interest is acceptable on a case by case basis. It is highly unlikely that living in a pub, even if your wife is the licence holder, will be acceptable.

"I had a County Court judgement against me but I have discharged the debt, am I ok to apply?"

Normally, people who have undischarged judgements against them will not be able to apply. If the debt is discharged an application from you will be considered.

"I was declared bankrupt 18 months ago can I apply to become a police officer?"

No. bankrupts will not be able to submit an application. The only way you can apply is if your bankruptcy has been discharged. You may be considered three years after discharge of the debt. You will need to provide a Certificate of Satisfaction with your application.

"I was convicted of GBH 15 years ago will I be able to apply to the police?"

You are likely to be rejected if you have been convicted of a serious crime like Grievous Bodily Harm (GBH). You should check the regulations and consult the force of your choice to see what is acceptable.

Medical Conditions

"I'm really worried that something will come up at my medical and I will be rejected. After getting through the Application and Assessment stages I will be really disappointed if I don't get in after all that I have achieved".

To alleviate any worries about the outcome of your medical, that often comes at the end of the process, you should make an appointment to see your general medical practitioner (GP) and explain that you intend to join the police. Ask if there is anything on your medical record that will be disclosed when the medical questionnaire is completed by the GP and if it is likely to cause a problem. If there is, deal with it and check with your chosen force what their position is with your condition. Sorting these things out before you apply prevents any worry and disappointment.

"I had my appendix out last year, will that be a problem?"
No. Normal invasive soft tissue surgery is not an issue providing you are fully recovered and there are no ongoing problems.

"I had my eyes lasered 12 months ago, is that likely to be a problem?"

No. The conditions around the recovery period following laser surgery have been relaxed considerably in recent years. Do check with your chosen force their requirements and how long they will wish you to recover before joining.

"My GP put me on antidepressants 2 years ago. It followed my Dad dying, getting divorced and being involved in a serious car accident. My whole world caved in. I only took them for about 9 months. Will that be a problem?"

The whole issue of depressive illness can create a problem for you. If you have a history of recurring illness over many years and you have been on medication you may find it difficult to join a police force. If you have had a single episode in your life when things have been really stressful and a short period of medical intervention has solved the problem, it is unlikely that it will create too much of a problem. The police will want to see some evidence that you are fully recovered and that you have been off medication for at least 6 months. As with all medical conditions you should check with your chosen force to check their policy.

"I had my anterior cruciate ligament (ACL) repaired in my right knee three years ago. I am now playing rugby again and fully fit. Will that be a problem getting into the police?"

Skeletal damage and tendon problems can be a problem. However, the Disability Discrimination Act 1995 (DDA) applies to the police service and your medical condition will be investigated. Providing there is no great risk of police work aggravating the condition or an early deterioration that could lead to medical retirement you should be fine. The most important thing you should do before you apply is to check with your specialist the current status of your condition and the likely prognosis. Then check with your chosen force whether they are likely to take you.

"My GP has records of me being diagnosed with asthma when I was only 10 years of age. I am now 27 and I have never had an attack but I am still prescribed an inhaler. Is this a problem?"

Asthma can cause you a problem if it is severe. Some people have an entry on their medical records that indicates they have asthma although they have never had an attack. It is possible that a GP can make the wrong diagnosis. When asthma is diagnosed it may be nothing more than hay fever. Police forces have different views on this medical condition but the best way forward is to check with your GP and consider being assessed again. A number of candidates have discovered they no longer have this condition. In fact, there have been examples of applicants who carry on normal lives and are extremely physically fit and compete in 'Iron Man' challenges and similar.

"I have got diabetes, can I join up?"

Providing you have your diabetes under control there is nothing to prevent you from applying. Whether you are Type 1 or Type 2 the police force will look carefully at your condition and assess whether you can be accommodated within the terms and conditions of the DDA. There may be restrictions placed on what you can do in terms of driving and use of firearms. Check with your chosen force to see what their position is in relation to your personal circumstances.

Application Form

"My handwriting and spelling are poor. Can I get a friend to fill in the form for me?"

No. It is clearly stated at the top of page 1 that you should "...complete all sections in person..." It is common sense that you should fill it in because it is about you and demonstrate that you can read and write.

"My Dad is a convicted burglar but I have not seen or heard of him for 15 years. Do I have to tell the police about him?"

Yes. You are required to tell the police as much information you know about your family members. It is important that you bear in mind the police request this information to ensure there is no undue influence brought to bear on you or the police service, whether family or otherwise. In this case you should state the facts as presented.

"Can I make up the answers to the competency based questions in Section 4 of the application form because I haven't got any good examples from my life experience?"

No. The purpose of Section 4 is to test whether you have the basic skills to be able to proceed to the Assessment Centre. You should use real life experiences and situations you have been involved in to illustrate your answers. Some candidates find this difficult. Take your time and think carefully about the experiences you have had and choose those which are most appropriate.

"If I don't tell the police I was cautioned when I was 14 for shoplifting, will that be a problem?"

Yes. The police will carry out extensive checks on you to determine whether you have ever been convicted of an offence or been involved in activities that could compromise your integrity. You should tell the police what you know about convictions. They will find out in any case and if you have not declared them they may assume you have not been totally honest. A childhood caution will not necessarily exclude you from becoming a police officer.

"How long will it be before I hear from the police after I have submitted my application form?"

This can vary from one force to another. Generally, you will hear fairly soon if you have failed to meet the basic entry criteria or failed to attain the pass mark in the competency questions in Section 4. Some forces like to carry out vetting checks before they are willing to send you forward to the Assessment Centre. This can take months. So, no news can be good news. You should check with your chosen force to be clear about the expected time scales. This will save unnecessary stress and repeated calls to the recruiting office seeking information.

"I don't want my current employer to know that I have applied to the police until I am certain that I will get in, what can I do about it because I know they will have to provide a reference?"

That's fine. The police will respect your wishes and will contact them when you are sure to get a job as a police officer. Just make sure you tick the appropriate box on the application form.

"Can I submit applications to four forces at the same time to see who will take me?"

No. You should pursue one application at a time. It is clear that you can only sit one Assessment Centre in a 12 month period. If you fail an assessment you must wait for six months before you can reapply.

"If I pass the Assessment Centre for one force can I change my mind and transfer the pass to another force?"

Some forces may be prepared to accept a transferred pass mark at the Assessment Centre because the selection process is national. If they do, be prepared for an interview. Many forces do not accept transferred pass marks. You should check with the force to which you wish to transfer before withdrawing from the force to which you first applied.

Assessment Centre

"What can I expect when I go to the Assessment Centre?"

You will attend either in the morning or afternoon and be there for about 5 hours. You should take a snack and drink with you because refreshments are not provided. You will be placed in a group of people who will move around the carousel of tests together. You will be tested on verbal and numerical skills, interact with a role actor to resolve four customer and staff issues, complete two written exercises and undergo a competency based interview.

"I have heard you should 'be yourself' when you go to the Assessment Centre?"

Yes, that is true. But, decide what that means after you have read the information about the Assessment Centre and the Westshire Centre Welcome Pack. You will be in role as a newly appointed Customer Services Officer in the four interactive scenarios and the two written exercises. You will have to behave and respond as if you were the real Customer Services Officer. So consider carefully how you will behave in this situation.

"I am good at Maths and English, so I will have no problem there?"

Just because you are good at Maths and English doesn't mean there is no need to practice. Many people assume they will have no problems and concentrate their energy on the other tests and do very badly at their Maths and English. Treat every test as an obstacle and make sure you can deal with it. This approach will increase your overall confidence.

"Can I use a calculator in the maths test?"

No.

"I have heard that you shouldn't worry about the core competencies – it's a matter of just getting on with what comes up?"

No. The 7 core competencies are fundamental to the Assessment Centre. You will be tested against them. You should take full advantage of the information that is provided to you before you attend. The competencies are clearly laid out with each defined, the standard required, the positive indicators and the negative indicators. You should be familiar with them all and have 'matched' yourself against them before you get there.

"In the interactive scenarios should I get a grip of the role actor and tell them how life is?"

No. That is not the way to deal with the scenarios. You must be professional, firm and fair. As a Customer Service Officer you are there to solve customer and staff problems. You must have a balanced approach, be sensitive to diversity issues, solve problems and look to dealing with the complaint in a way that will attempt to satisfy the person you are dealing with.

"Should I worry about the 'Westshire Centre Welcome Pack' before I get to the assessment centre or just use it when I am there?"

The Westshire Centre Welcome Pack is very important. It is sent to you to prepare yourself before attending the Assessment Centre. It is the pieces of the 'jigsaw puzzle' that you have to deal with. It gives you almost everything you will need to deal effectively with the exercises. The role actors and the briefing information you will be given on the day will provide the final piece of the jigsaw. It is very important that you familiarise yourself with the pack.

"Can't see any reason to get all dressed up to go through the centre; I didn't get dressed up for university finals, what do you think?"

First impressions count. You are seeking to impress the assessors because you want to become a police officer. Police officers set standards in society through integrity and image. You should dress in a suit and look professional. Also, remember that you will be in role as a Customer Service Officer and you are fronting the highest possible standards of customer care.

"What is the pass mark for the Assessment Centre?"

The overall pass mark is 60%. However, it is obligatory that you score 60% in Respect for Race and Diversity, 60% in Oral Communication and 44% in Written Communication. It is possible to score 66% overall and fail because you only score 33% in Written Communication. You need to be well prepared and perform well across all the exercises. Some police forces have reduced the overall pass mark to marks below 60% to meet local requirements. You should check with your chosen force to confirm the pass mark.

"I have heard diversity is a big issue at these assessments?"

Diversity is a big issue and you need to understand what it is about and how you demonstrate that you are sensitive to the issues. In every exercise you will be tested on your sensitivity to issues around the competency Respect for Race and Diversity. Also, if you fail to achieve a pass mark of 60% in this area you will fail. You should familiarise yourself with the current issues.

"At the interview will I be asked questions on a broad range of topics and should I take my application form in case they ask me questions about it?"

The competency based interview is not a broad ranging interview that you may have experienced in the past. You will be asked 4 questions on 4 competencies and have 5 minutes to answer each one. Currently, they are Respect for Race and Diversity, Team Working, Resilience and Personal Responsibility. You will not be asked about any other issues, including your application form.

"My force has a 'filter interview' that you have to go through if you pass the Assessment Centre, what is that like?"

A 'Filter Interview' is a panel interview with two or three members who will have a remit to ask you broad ranging questions like: 'Why do you want to join this force?' or 'What papers do you read?' In this type of interview you can expect many different questions and is very different from the NRM Competency Based Interview that is restricted to 4 questions on the given competencies.

"When do I get my results and feed back from the assessment?"

About two weeks after you have attended the Assessment Centre.

About ISP Consultancy

Ian Hutchison

ISP Consultancy was established by Ian Hutchison following a career with Thames Valley Police.

After military service in the mid 1970s he joined the police service and pursued an exciting and challenging career during which he was promoted though the ranks to Chief Superintendent.

He served at various places across the Thames Valley gaining wide policing experience including working in urban and rural areas, managing major police operations, working on national policing projects and leading the Serious Crime Squad in surveillance and investigation of major crime.

He is a law graduate, has masters in criminology, is a Fellow of the Chartered Management Institute and a member of the British Psychological Society.

ISP Consultancy

ISP Consultancy is a highly professional and experienced training organisation that specialises in assisting people to join the police service.

We are the only company in the U.K. that offers comprehensive training for potential police recruits. We will assist you in the preliminary stages when you are considering a police career, take you through the police national selection process and, after appointment as a constable, assist you with career progression.

Joining the police service is one of the most important life decisions you will make. It is essential you get it right. To assist you we provide:

- aptitude testing for police work - try our free web based test
- assistance with the application process
- one day development courses
- half-day seminars
- one-to-one coaching
- interview techniques courses

Our development courses and seminars are run at locations across the country.

All of our graduates pass Stage 1 (Application) and Stage 2 (Assessment Centre). We are proud of our high pass rate. We routinely achieve some of the highest pass marks in the country – 72%, 74%, 75%, 76%, 78% and 80%!

We also pride ourselves in striking a personal relationship with our clients. You are not just a client; you will become a friend of ISP and we that will act as your mentor and source of guidance as your career progresses.

After you are appointed as a serving police officer we will assist you with your career development so that you can get into a specialist role, pass promotion selection boards or get you on the High Potential Development Scheme.

We also work with police forces across the country helping officers with personal development, team working and leadership. We operate inside and outside the police service so we are aware of developments in policing and the impact on police officers.

The Courses and Services

Application Form

The Application Form is the first stage in the selection process. It requires you to provide a considerable amount of personal information to enable the police to determine whether you fit the recruitment criteria. In addition, the application form contains 8 questions that you will have to answer. The first 4 questions are 'Competency Based Questions' (CBQ) that require you to provide answers demonstrating you have the basic life experiences and skills to enable your progression to the Assessment Centre stage. After submitting the application the answers are marked and graded 'A', 'B', 'C' or 'D'. To pass the application stage you will have to attain a grade 'B', or higher, overall. If you fail this first stage of the process you will have to wait 6 months before you can reapply.

It goes without saying that you must take the greatest care in completing the application form and, in particular, formulating your answers to the 4 competency based questions.

Many people fail at this stage because they do not understand what is required.

ISP will assist you to understand what is required and advise you accordingly. We do not fill in the application for you, tell you what to write or what phrases and words to use. If we did that it would be unethical and you would be submitting an application, which is not yours! However, we will help you understand the general principles and how to discover suitable life experiences that will evidence the competencies required.

All of our applicants that take advantage of this assistance go through to the assessment stage.

Police Selection Development Course

The Police Selection Development Course (PSDC) has two objectives.

- To explain the challenge of the police selection assessment centre.
- To provide you with a 'tool kit' that you can use to develop your skills over the months leading up to your assessment.

You will learn how to match yourself to the core competencies and how to approach the individual exercises you will have to undertake.

The course will provide everything you need to know about the process and you will have an opportunity to understand and practice, in a safe environment, your team skills, the scenarios, written exercises and the interview. You should not feel apprehensive about the day because it is designed to be fun!

We know from experience that the secret to success is more than just understanding what is required; it is in your ability to 'demonstrate' the skills.

Techniques for dealing with the numerical and verbal reasoning tests will be explained.

You will also receive a comprehensive Study Pack that you will take away with you to reinforce your learning.

The course enables you to network with other applicants and, after the course ISP will support you through the process with advice and guidance.

A tutorial in the afternoon provides an opportunity to discuss your future development. Our experience is that the course lives up to the two stated objectives and delegates quickly become aware of what development they need to reach the standard required. The tutorial will focus on your key development areas.

All the courses have a balanced number of delegates because we recognise the importance of allowing you to maximise your learning in the time available. The course is relaxed, fun and designed so you will be prepared for the selection process.

Development Seminars

Between the Police Selection Development Course and your assessment date you will have pursued your development plan and had an opportunity to deal with some of the key issues raised by the course. In consequence, you will have improved in many areas and increased your chances of success at the Assessment Centre.

To make sure your development is maintained and you achieve a good pass mark it is essential to take advantage of our intensive training.

Prior to every national assessment session we run a series of half day seminars and one-to-one coaching. The seminars are a great way of learning and practising with a small group of other candidates. You will learn from each other and gain the confidence to know you can achieve well beyond the standard required. If you are unable to attend the seminars or you need more development work, one-to-one sessions will be available to you.

The seminars run six weeks prior to each of the Assessment Centre sessions on Saturday mornings from 9 am until 1 pm.

Demonstration DVD

To complement the skills learned on the Police Selection Development Course, the Development Seminars and this book a demonstration DVD is available. Two potential police recruits illustrate what will be required of you at the Assessment Centre in the Interactive Scenarios and the Competency Based Interview. This is essential viewing for all potential recruits to enable you to understand and assimilate the seven point plan and the structured interview. The DVD can be purchased through our web site www.ispconsultancy.com.

Interview Techniques

The police service is always seeking to identify the most highly motivated and skilled people to fill promotion vacancies, specialist posts and place future leaders on the High Potential Development Scheme (HPDS).

Most selection processes incorporate some form of presentation or assessment centre whether you are seeking promotion, a specialist post or a place on the HPDS.

The common feature, in nearly all cases, is the **Selection Interview Board**.

At some point you will have to sit in front of a panel, answer questions and tell them about yourself. This is the hardest step for most people, is often intimidating and can feel as if the whole process is shrouded in mystery.

ISP Interview Techniques training is designed to demystify the board process and prepare you for the challenge. The training is delivered as a single day course or as a package tailored for individuals and explains how you should prepare for the big day and how to deal with the practical aspects of the interview. You will learn the fundamentals of:

- Team working
- Principles of effective management
- Discovering your personality
- Matching personality to role & strategy
- Setting the agenda for the interview
- Dealing with topics
- Answering questions
- Structuring your preparation
- Developing leadership behaviours
- Managing the practicalities of the interview

Practical exercises and demonstrations are combined with a wealth of experience to present an unforgettable learning experience. In addition, you will receive a comprehensive Study Pack and be supported with advice and guidance.

The courses have a balanced number of delegates to allow you to maximise your learning in the time available. Overall, the training is relaxed, fun and designed so you can prepare yourself for the selection interview.

These skills only need to be learned once. You will reap the benefits throughout your career For more information take a look at our web site:

www.ispconsultancy.com

Testimonials

Testimonials

Here is a sample of what some of our satisfied customers have said about the services we provide:

"Preparation is the key. I was 110% prepared and the course gave me the confidence I needed, it is priceless! Thanks, Ian"
J S

"I do feel the course has prepared me well. I was surprised how many people had come from different areas of the country. The group size was good".
MJ

"ISP helped me through the selection process for the police by not only showing me what I needed to do but what not to do. Ian and his staff were always on hand with expert guidance throughout the process for me and the other candidates. I learned what to expect and how to deal with it

and had a lot of fun in the process. I would recommend ISP to anyone thinking of applying for the police"
SW

"Thank you so much for all your help with preparing me for interview. I feel that the work we did together directly benefited me. I felt more confident to clearly structure and articulate answers"
MR

"Thank you for all your help...your sessions have been invaluable to me and have given me the confidence to achieve my dream. Thank you once again"
KW

"Even one session with Ian will leave you feeling confident and prepared for the whole recruitment process"
RO

"Great feed back from others and ideas with the team role exercise. I feel confident to go forward and develop myself with some home work"
RB

"I feel far more prepared having attended this course than anything I have read on the internet or been told by other applicants and police officers. I feel I can build upon what I have learned today and hopefully pass the selection process. The course exceeded my expectations. An excellent day. Great group of people. Good

moving on of subjects, not dwelling on certain aspects too much. Not boring. Really good day"
H R

"Fantastic! Very thorough and informative. You have given me a whole new level of confidence. Money well spent!"
LK

"Very beneficial, was very nervous about coming beforehand but it was a good relaxed atmosphere that instantly put me at ease. I feel far more prepared and feel happier knowing what to work on for the actual assessment. Have been given plenty of food for thought!"
JO

"ISP is an exceptional company. Ian's unwavering commitment to extracting the best from his pupils ensures nothing but success. With his support, guidance and expertise I have not only realised my ambition to join the police force but gained a good friend"
GP

Printed in the United Kingdom
by Lightning Source UK Ltd.
132105UK00001B/4-36/P